BEADING
by Machine

OTHER BOOKS OF INTEREST FROM CHILTON BOOK COMPANY

BEADING
by Machine

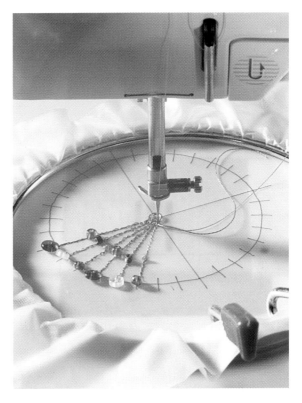

YVONNE PEREZ-COLLINS

ILLUSTRATIONS BY
MARY ELLEN SZPER

RADNOR, PENNSYLVANIA

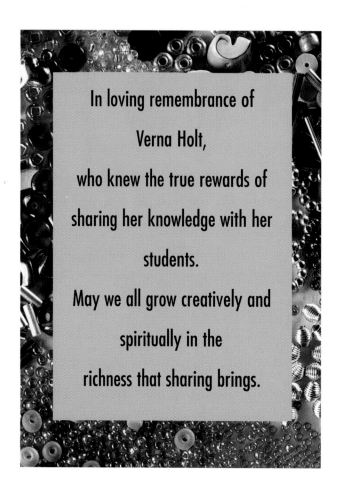

In loving remembrance of

Verna Holt,

who knew the true rewards of

sharing her knowledge with her

students.

May we all grow creatively and

spiritually in the

richness that sharing brings.

Published in Radnor, Pennsylvania 19089 by Chilton Book Company

Designed by Anthony Jacobson
Photography by Donna Chiarelli

Manufactured in the United States of America

Library of Congress Cataloging-in-Publication Data

Perez-Collins, Yvonne.
    Beading by machine / Yvonne Perez-Collins : illustrations by Mary
Ellen Szper.
       p.   cm.
    Includes bibliographical references and index.
    ISBN 0-8019-8642-7
    1. Beadwork.   2. Machine sewing.   I. Title.
TT860.P47   1997
746.5—dc 20   96-46069
                                        CIP

1 2 3 4 5 6 7 8 9 0   6 5 4 3 2 1 0 9 8 7

CONTENTS

Part 3 LET'S BEAD!

INTRODUCTION

Pack your supply bags for a tour of the world of beading by machine! Relax, enjoy, and let this book be your guide. Besides charting the basics of your journey—beads, tools, supplies, and techniques—I provide many tips and tricks to help make all your future beading adventures successful. Always I encourage you to learn and practice what I have mapped out and then, when you feel comfortable, stray confidently from the charted course.

This book presents techniques and projects designed specifically for beading by sewing machine. Some have been adapted from traditional hand sewing methods, while others spring from nothing more than imagination, innovation, and experimentation, both mine and that of other beading artists. The book is divided into three parts. The first part, "Get Ready," pertains to beading in general. It discusses selecting, buying, and crafting beads and also provides some basics about tools and important techniques such as tying knots. The second part of the book, "Get Set," introduces the sewing machine into the beading picture. This part helps you decide what to bead on your sewing machine and then explains how to set up your machine for machine beading. It also describes tools and materials that are particularly useful for machine beading and what general steps to take when beading by machine. The title of the third part says it all: "Let's Bead!" The chapters in this part describe specific machine beading techniques and offer projects to help you master the techniques. The step-by-step instructions will allow you to create lovely jewelry and gifts for yourself and your family and friends. Creating something beautiful is fulfilling. Combining materials, tools, and techniques to produce something one-of-a-kind is rewarding, in terms of both the physical product that results and the creative process that allows for self-expression. As Robert Liu, editor of *Ornament* magazine states, "Art is a record of a new idea. Art is the product of the eye and the mind." The longevity of your machine-beaded creations is determined by the quality of the beads, materials, and construction methods you choose. Historical pieces of beadwork have lasted for centuries, and it is gratifying to realize that if you do your work carefully, your work can last—and be enjoyed—for ages.

With great admiration I offer my thanks to all the beading artists, past and present, who have added to the rich body of beading techniques. I would especially like to offer recognition to those who teach beadwork to others, preserving old beading traditions, creating new beading traditions, and passing on the inspiration to bead.

Part 1
GET READY

Are you ready to get ready? While this first part of the book does not talk about machine beading at all, it is an important place to begin your journey into the world of beading by machine. The first chapter gives you bead basics—where to buy, sizes, materials, and so on—and also encourages you to craft your own using various techniques and materials. While there are nearly countless types of beads you can buy, from semiprecious stones to sliced shells to fragrant beads made from ground spices, there is something uniquely satisfying about expressing yourself through beads you make yourself, "from scratch."

Chapter 2 is your toolbox, a handy collection of useful information and ideas you'll want to read at least once before you get started beading. In this chapter you'll find options for lighting your work space, suggestions for storing and organizing your beads, basic instructions for tying various useful knots, and needle and threading information, as well as expert tips and ideas to help make your beading enjoyable and your beadwork durable.

Chapter 1
• • • • • • • • • •

BEADS, BEADS, BEADS

Let's start with a fresh view of beads. While most people might think of a bead as being a small round object with a hole in the center, a quick walk through any bead store reveals that beads aren't necessarily small or round—and the hole isn't always in the center. Let's consider anything with a hole as fair game for beading.

This chapter shows you many ways to craft your own beads using art supplies and various items found around the house. You can make round beads if you take a conservative approach to crafting, or you can make a creative statement by crafting original beads with unusual shapes and textures.

ORNAMENTATION FOR ALL TIMES

Beads are among the oldest art forms in the world. Their use for ornamentation, trading, and status has been important throughout history. In 1626, for example, beads were part of what the Dutch paid local Indians for the island of Manhattan. Many things have changed over the centuries, but beads and beadwork are still valued and desirable today. Finding, owning, and handling beads is particularly fulfilling to avid beaders.

There are beads to capture the interest of any designer or collector. Every kind of bead—African trade, lampwork, Baltic amber, carved bone, Czechoslovakian glass, carved fetish—has its own charm and distinctive style. There is a lot of history associated with beads, and through the years they have been a revealing and inspiring symbol of humanity's most basic cultural and spiritual aspirations. *Collectible Beads: A Universal Aesthetic*, by Robert K. Liu, discusses this universal symbolism as well as the worldwide growth over the last 20 years of collecting ancient and contemporary beads. Our fascination with beads is not surprising when you realize that they are more than just the stuff they are made of. They appeal to almost everyone, from those with the simplest tastes to those with the most exotic tastes. In a way, they are the story of us all.

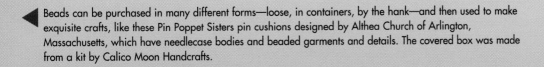

◀ Beads can be purchased in many different forms—loose, in containers, by the hank—and then used to make exquisite crafts, like these Pin Poppet Sisters pin cushions designed by Althea Church of Arlington, Massachusetts, which have needlecase bodies and beaded garments and details. The covered box was made from a kit by Calico Moon Handcrafts.

BUYING BEADS

Beads can be purchased in various quantities: individually, by weight, prepackaged in small amounts, in plastic storage containers containing 1 ounce of beads (500 seed beads), by the 10″ to 34″ strand, by the hank (ten 18″ strands), or by the kilo (loose beads). There are many sources for beads for your projects. Craft stores and bead stores are the obvious places to start, but don't forget to check out old jewelry at yard sales (overlooked treasure!) and catalogs for bead supply houses. To request catalogs, consult *The Bead Directory* (see References) or look for addresses in beading magazines. If you have a computer and are connected to the Internet, you can find some informative and interesting sources via that avenue.

The size of seed beads is sometimes written with a number followed by a degree sign or a degree sign with a line below it. This is an abbreviation for "aught" (zero), which once was the beginning of an arbitrary size scale that started at zero and increased as the size increased. Beads smaller than "aughts" were designated with multiple zeros, and soon it was easier to write 11° instead of writing 11 zeros. The most common designation for seed bead sizes, which is similar to the previous approach, is a number followed by a slash and a zero: for example, 11/0. Note that pearls, semiprecious stones, and many other beads are commonly sized by millimeters rather than aughts. Also note that it is the *size of the hole* in the beads that matters when you are beading—particularly machine beading—not the size of the bead itself.

Hole sizes can vary in apparently same-size glass beads, even if they come from the same lot. Hole sizes are the most consistent in Japanese beads like Delica and Antique beads where the bead size is uniform and the large holes allow for several stitches to pass through. The holes in relatively small semiprecious stones are smaller than holes in the larger beads of the same type and thus require finer thread for stringing.

"NON-BEADS" TO CONSIDER

One visit to the bead store or five minutes with a bead catalog will be enough to make you realize, "So many beads, so little time!" Sometimes I wonder if a time bandit hides in my stash of beads and steals away the time when I get ready to bead. With countless sizes, colors, and kinds of beads available, you might wonder why we should bother to look elsewhere for beads. Well, why not? Creativity is a noble pursuit. Consider the possibilities: Almost anything with a hole is a potential bead. As long as the object is less than ¼″ thick and the hole is large enough for a machine needle to pass through, you can attach it with the sewing machine. For example, miniature puzzle pieces can become dangles for earrings if you punch a hole in them with an awl.

Items such as coins, keys, flip-tops from aluminum cans, washers, tokens, and watch parts are bead possibilities. A visit to the hardware store with a new outlook might garner beading treasures at a low price (Figure 1.1). There's a certain thrill to doing something and saying to yourself, "I wonder if anyone's ever done *this* before!"

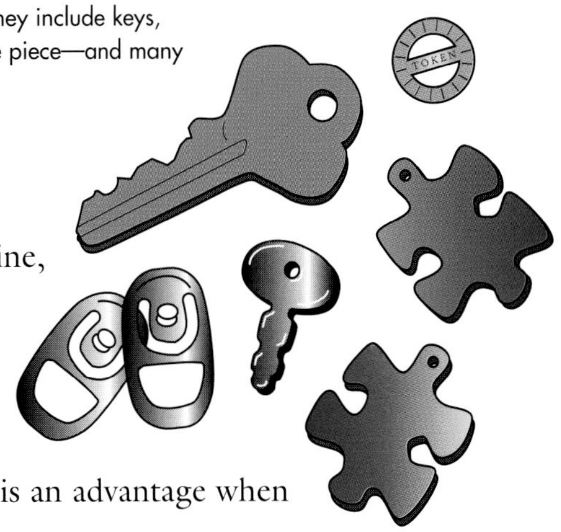

Figure 1.1 These "non-beads" are items that can be strung as charms. They include keys, tokens, and flip-tops from aluminum cans. A hole can be made in a puzzle piece—and many other items—with an awl.

CRAFTING BEADS

The emphasis of this book is on beading by machine, but I also want to share some ways for you to make your own exciting beads. Sometimes it is easiest to start with an actual bead and cover it with different things, creating texture. Wooden beads are good bases since they are light and most glues will adhere easily. The ease of painting, gluing, and dyeing wood is an advantage when crafting your own beads.

You will find an array of paints and sealants at art and craft stores. Check such features as waterproofness, cleanup requirements, and ventilation to help you select one to fit your needs. Some products have few or no noticeable fumes and need only water for cleanup, while others require good ventilation in the work area and must be cleaned up with solvents. Be sure to follow the manufacturer's instructions.

Rub 'N Buff by AMACO is a fine wax metallic finish that is simply applied with your finger to plastic, metal, wood, or fiber surfaces. The lightest application brings beads and findings to life. With 18 colors to choose from, you can give character to your "duds," making all your creations usable. I use Rub 'N Buff to rescue glue gun beads (described later in this chapter) whose color combinations are undesirable. AMACO's Brush 'N Leaf is a liquid formula that can be applied with a brush into textured surfaces, like antiquing.

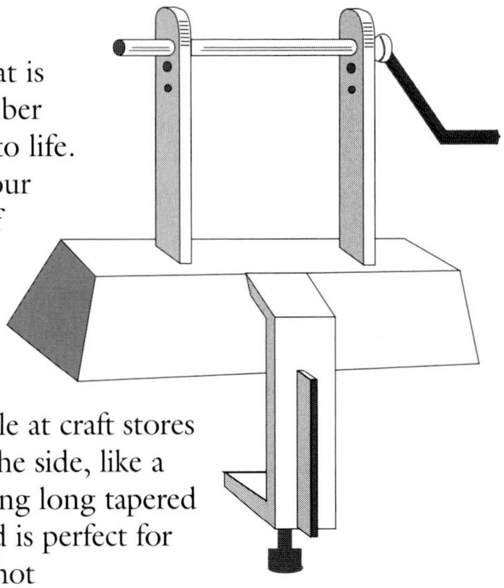

A handy tool for bead making is the Craft Beader, available at craft stores (Figure 1.2). It has a horizontal pole turned by a handle on the side, like a miniature rotisserie. The Craft Beader was designed for winding long tapered strips of paper into beads. It clamps to the edge of a table and is perfect for making beads in other mediums, too, like polymer clays and hot glue. With this tool, you can make winding assemblages of hot glue and threads (discussed later in this chapter). Start with a wooden bead or a rolled paper bead for the basic shape. If the bead hole is too large for the spindle, insert a small piece of cardboard in the split of the spindle, on both sides of the bead.

Figure 1.2 The Craft Beader is a tool that clamps to a table and can be used when crafting beads. The bead goes on the spindle, which rotates the bead while glue or paint is being applied.

I also like to turn beads (that I am painting or crafting) on the tapered end of an African porcupine quill (Figure 1.3). Such quills can be purchased at bead stores. A quill is about the length of a pencil and will hold almost any size of bead on its long tapered ends. Poke a piece of pencil eraser over each point to protect yourself and the point.

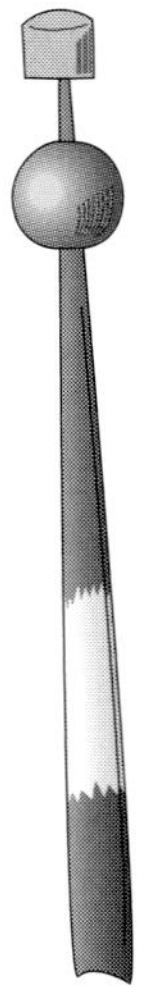

Figure 1.3 A porcupine quill is useful for holding beads as you decorate them, because its tapered end fits many sizes of beads. A piece of pencil eraser on each end protects the point.

Aggregate Beads

Aggregate beads are made by covering a bead with tiny objects to give texture or color. You can use a wooden bead or a reject polymer bead as a gluing base, or, for a featherweight base, try a small Styrofoam ball. For unusual shapes, make your own beads from modeling compounds such as Model Magic by Liquitex or Creative Paperclay. The beads air-dry in 24 hours and are very light, making them ideal for earrings and large beads.

Here are some of the supplies you might wish to use for bead crafting:

polymer clay
cornmeal
mustard seeds
scented rice or wax beads from bath shops
sealing wax and seed beads
rayon and metallic threads and cords
layers of tissue paper
Japanese Washi paper
colored or metallic glue sticks designed for glue guns
cord or braids

Most aggregate beads can be painted with acrylic paint or sealed with a clear glaze. Applying a thick, clear glaze will add depth to the texture and will seal the finish so it is waterproof. You can even use special clear glazes that add a glittery sparkle.

Food Beads

Food beads should not be sewn on garments, but they are great for purely decorative items and jewelry. Remember, almost anything can be a bead! I discovered a neat shrunken texture on frozen peas that had been cooked and then air-dried; the peas made interesting beads when drilled, painted, and sealed with a glaze. You can also string multicolored Indian corn, after carefully breaking the kernels off the cob. Soak the kernels in water for about a day until they are soft enough to be threaded with a needle; when stringing them, use heavy cord, elastic cord, or a strong synthetic thread.

DYED MACARONI BEADS

These may not sound exciting, but you'll gain a new respect for macaroni beads once you see how easily the different shapes can be dyed to obtain brilliant hues. Dried macaroni sold with cheese sauce is available in dinosaur, musical instrument, and cartoon shapes. Kitchen and gourmet stores often carry pasta formed in seasonal shapes, such as pumpkins, Christmas trees, bunnies, hearts, clovers, stars, and flags. Some shapes are plain, while others are colored with spinach or tomato. Here I'll show you two good methods for dyeing pasta whatever colors you choose.

METHOD 1—For each color, pour ¼ cup of rubbing alcohol into a small glass jar, such as a baby food jar. Add food coloring until the solution reaches the desired shade, about 15 to 20 drops. (I discovered Dr. Ph. Martin's Radiant Concentrated Water Color in an art store and found that its colors—a broad selection—dye the pasta beautifully.) I start by dyeing some pasta with a light color and then add 5 to 8 drops to dye another batch. You can use the same alcohol to dye batches in several gradations of the original color. Eventually you can combine one batch of dye with another for the final dark color; for example, you can mix reds with blues to obtain a rich purple. The alcohol-dye solution will retain its intensity until the last drop is used.

Keep the uncooked macaroni in the jar of dye for 10 minutes, then spread it on a cookie sheet lined with a double layer of paper towels, where it will dry quickly. The pasta shapes can be sprayed with any clear protective coating. Krylon's Illinois Bronze Crystal Clear Glaze creates a triple-thick glaze equal to three coats, giving a glass-like finish.

METHOD 2—Another way to color dried macaroni is to put it in a plastic bag with powdered tempera paint and shake the bag. The pasta absorbs the color beautifully, but the excess powder needs to be removed so that stringing isn't too messy. Sealing the string of macaroni with a protective spray coating will protect the color. Krylon's Crystal Clear Acrylic Coating works well, as does its Satin Finish.

Plastic Charms

You can make clear plastic charms using Aleene's Shrink-It Plastic, invented in 1973. This clear plastic is found in most craft stores. When baked in the oven, the cut shapes made from this material will turn opaque and will reduce to one-fourth of their original size, remaining flat or becoming slightly domed. Follow manufacturer's instructions for baking. You can draw on the plastic with a felt pen to create details, coloring in whole areas, if desired; do both sides, so the charm is not one-sided. Note that if you want the edges to be colored you must color them carefully with your marker before baking so they do not appear white after the piece shrinks. Before baking, you can remove permanent ink (and regular ink) from the plastic with an ordinary pencil eraser if you need to. For a neat effect, shapes can be shrunk with a thin layer of glue sprinkled with embossing powder, like that used for rubber stamping. Before baking, make stringing holes in the plastic with a paper punch or a hole punch made for leather. Marvy/Uchida's Jumbo Craft Punches are perfect for cutting out charms; such charms will shrink to about ⅜″.

If you can't find Aleene's Shrink-It or you're really in a crafting mood, you can make charms from clear plastic deli containers, although the quality won't be quite as good. Begin by lightly sanding the plastic with a fine grit sandpaper or a pot scrubber so that paint, ink, or pencil will adhere to the plastic better. Sharpie pens will make thick lines and Sakura's Pigma pens will make ultra-fine lines if you want to write or draw details. Many plastics used in packaging (like that used for greeting card box covers) will shrink and curl significantly when baked in an oven. Heavier deli containers or clear cake covers from store-bought cakes produce flatter pieces.

Preheat the oven 275° to 300° F. Bake on a foil-lined or nonstick baking pan. Be sure to check every minute to see if the pieces are shrinking. The approximate cooking time is less than 10 minutes. The shapes will lie flat if you pull them out right away. If necessary, they can be flattened by covering them with foil and placing a book on top. Curling and distortion occurs when the plastic is thin or the shapes are cooked longer than necessary. Pieces cannot be reheated to flatten.

Fiber Beads

These lightweight swirls of color are made from assorted thread scraps, so this technique offers you a great way to use up odd bits of thread on bobbins and old spools. Coat a handful of threads with any nontoxic craft glue that dries clear. Roll the threads into a ball about ½" across and let it sit for a minute. Roll the beads again every few minutes so the threads will conform to a shape as the glue dries. Although it is not necessary, the beads can be clear-coated with a matte or gloss finish.

Another style of thread bead is made by wrapping an existing bead with several strands of threads at the same time. Apply glue to the first 10" of a bundle of 5 to 10 threads so they are saturated and will adhere to each other while you are wrapping. These beads also can be coated with matte or gloss finish.

You can make felt beads by rolling a pinch of carded wool between the palms of your hands as you would do with a ball of clay. First rub a bar of soap on wet hands so the wool will slide on your hands easily as it rolls and compacts. Using multiple colors of wool will produce swirls of colors. These felted beads can be threaded onto yarn with a darning needle.

Glue Gun Beads

I enjoy making beads using the wide range of colors of glue that are available, such as those made by Tecnocraft. There is glue on the market in pastel, primary, glitter, and neon colors—and even glow-in-the-dark!

Shown here (from left to right) are some loose dyed macaroni beads in whimsical shapes, a thread necklace and matching earrings by Bambi Stalder, a necklace made from felted wool by Anne Vickrey, a necklace made from glue gun beads, and some finely detailed polymer beads by Z. Kripke.

To begin, use lotion on your hands to prevent the hot glue from sticking in case it contacts your skin. The glue-beads start with a paper, plastic, or wooden bead for a base. I apply colors of glue by inserting ½″ lengths of different colors into the gun. I like to use the smaller, ¼″-diameter glue sticks since they are easily cut with wire cutters. If necessary, insert a full-length stick at the end to keep the short pieces feeding smoothly—it can be pulled out to insert more colors. Avid glue-crafters might have more than one glue gun in use at the same time with different colors in each one. At a few dollars each, it is an efficient and inexpensive option.

For turning a bead while gluing it, you can either mount it on the long tapered end of a pen (or African porcupine quill) or use the Craft Beader, described earlier in this chapter. If you use the Craft Beader, choose one of the three spindles closest to the hole size of the bead.

Hot glue makes long strands every time the nozzle of the gun touches an object. In most projects this is a bother, but here it is the key to making unusual beads. By using a repeated touch-lift-touch technique and continuously feeding the glue through the gun, you can make a random pattern so the short (¼″) strings crisscross each other, building up layers until the bead is the desired size. Another method also uses the touch-lift-touch technique, but the strings of glue are about ⅜″ long and all run in the same direction, around the bead. They build up layers and create depth in the design.

TIPS AND IDEAS FOR GLUE GUN BEADS

- Push beads and findings into the warm glue.
- Put Delta's Jewel Glue into the crevices and fill with beads.
- Set rhinestones and metal trims in cooled glue-beads with a Beadazzler or BeJeweler tool (these tools grasp and heat the trim, which is backed with glue).
- Wrap novelty yarns and metallic threads around the glue-beads, embedding them in the glue. Glue-beads can be reheated with the tip of the glue gun.
- Cut novelty shapes for charms out of a thin layer of cooled glue using Marvy/Uchida's Jumbo Craft punches. First squeeze glue out on a nonstick work surface (for example, Tecnocraft's UNI Pad). Immediately cover with a second pad and apply even pressure with a heavy rolling pin to make a thin layer of glue. Shapes may be cut out with scissors or craft punches.

Polymer Clay Beads

Polymer clay is a nongreasy, malleable clay that will not harden until it is baked. Some of the techniques used on polymer beads, such as making canes, are borrowed from Venetian glass making. When making canes, several colors of clay are assembled into a block to create a pattern or image in the sliced cross-section. Rolling and stretching the cane reduces the size of the pattern. In millefiori designs (literally, "a thousand flowers"), slices of the canes expose a pattern or picture.

Before baking, polymer clay can be embedded with sequins, glass, metals, feathers, beads, or jewelry findings, and it can even be enhanced with gold leaf. Inserting small wire loops before baking will give you places to attach fringe, fibers, or findings.

The average curing time for polymer clay in a household oven is about 20 minutes at 270°F. This varies with different brands of clay and with the size (and thickness) of the project. The clay can also be hardened by placing the finished object in a heated crock pot filled with water and leaving it in for at least 20 minutes. The advantages to this method are (1) you don't have to keep going to the oven to cook your beads and (2) leaving them in for a few hours won't hurt them (they won't burn). One drawback is that the clay acquires a powdered finish unless it is clear-coated after cooking. As with other polymer clay tools and equipment, the crock should not be used with food thereafter.

Some polymer clays require kneading to make them pliable, and a popular method is to dedicate a small food processor to this task. Hand-crank pasta machines help to roll out smooth layers and assist in blending colors. Another quick way to soften polymer clay was discovered by Cristofer Aven, a photo/fiber artist from Hayward, California. To use his method you need an electric palm sander that is normally used on wood. Instead of using sandpaper, cover the sanding pad with a piece of Reynolds freezer paper (shiny side showing). This paper will wear out and will need to be changed for each color of clay. Put the clay on a Teflon cookie sheet with a towel underneath to protect the work surface from the vibrating pan. The clay will start to soften in less than a minute. Turn it over and vibrate some more. Older clays and some colors like metallics may need a drop of mineral oil to help them become soft.

If you end up with polymer beads whose colors aren't usable, the beads can be salvaged. Simply apply new layers of clay and cook the beads again or else use the ideas in the section entitled "Aggregate Beads" (earlier in this chapter) to help save "failed" polymer beads.

If those methods aren't what you're looking for, perhaps it is time to take out your paints! Put a baked bead on the end of a quill or tapered pen. Paint the bead any way you like. You can use Krylon's brilliant Metallic Spray Paints to achieve the look of shiny metals—silver, gold, brass, or copper. If metals aren't your thing, try using Krylon's Stone Craft, Marble Craft, or Illinois Bronze Webbing Spray (or other types of craft paint) to completely cover the original color. Poke the quill (or pen) into a piece of Styrofoam while the painted bead dries.

Refer to the References and the Resources section for other information on the subject of polymer clay. The information from these books will save you the anguish of ruined projects by providing tips on how to make the process a success, and the ideas from experienced clay workers are inspiring. If you are interested in making your own clays, see MaryAnn Kohl's book, *Mudworks,* which presents over 100 recipes, under such headings as cooked/uncooked dough, playdough, baked/dried bread dough, and plaster of Paris.

Glass Beads

MAKING GLASS BEADS

Lewis Wilson, known for his dragon beads, has produced four videos on bead making. He teaches classes at his school, the New Mexico Glass Adventure, in Albuquerque. His inspiring outlook: "Make a bead—be happy." He would like to sit two world leaders at the same table and teach them how to make a glass bead. He is sure they would be so engrossed in the wonders of lampwork that they wouldn't have time to think about war and making bombs!

If you would like to learn about making glass beads, refer to the Resources section at the back of this book; many bead shops and craft schools offer classes on this subject.

ETCHING GLASS BEADS

You might have a project using glass beads for which you want to use two or three matte shades of one color or you want to blend gloss and matte beads. You can give almost any glass bead or button a permanent matte finish by soaking it in Dip 'N Etch by B & B Products, Inc. I suggest using this etching product because of its approval by the Art and Craft Materials Institute and because of its nonacid, odorless formula. In addition, it is reusable. A thicker cream version of the same formula, B & B Etching Creme, can be used for painting; it allows for better control on curved and vertical surfaces. Intricate lines and dot patterns can be applied by using B & B Etching Creme in small squeeze bottles with a Tip-Pen on the end. Tip-Pens are fine metal tips that screw onto the tip of plastic squeeze bottles. The four available sizes have the precision of technical pens.

I recommend testing a few beads and recording the results before dipping your entire supply. Put several beads in the etching liquid. After five minutes begin checking your beads at one-minute intervals until you get the effect and color you want. Use a plastic container for the etching liquid and stir occasionally with a plastic utensil. After removing the beads, rinse them under running water and then wash them in soapy water. By varying soaking times from five to fifteen minutes you can produce a gradation of shades from a light etch to a solid opaque. *Note:* Do not rinse the beads in a porcelain sink because the etching solution may damage (etch) such sinks and ceramic tile; use a large metal pot or a plastic bucket for rinsing if all your sinks are porcelain.

Handmade glass beads may not react to the etching if they are high-fired or have a high lead content. As with any glass beads, experiment and document the results so you can duplicate the effects you like. Etching can be a solution for salvaging scratched glass pieces. Note that entire necklaces can be dipped without damage to the string, chain, or metal findings, and you may choose to prestring selected beads for easy removal from Dip 'N Etch. When etching loose beads, pour them into a strainer lined with a nylon stocking while returning the etching liquid to its container.

Etching glass beads gives you a unique way to sign, identify, or decorate your work. After etching your design, you can add metallic details using Rub 'N Buff by AMACO. Simply rub it on with your fingertip and then polish the bead with a soft cloth. The color will permanently adhere to the etched surface. Rub 'N Buff adheres to the etched areas only and can be wiped right off the smooth sections. Eighteen metallic colors offer exciting possibilities for glass beads and buttons. Note that gentle hand washing is suggested for garments with glass items attached.

Chapter 2

•••••••••••

TIPS, TOOLS, & MATERIALS

Let's start by organizing your supplies and work area—this will help you to have a clear mind when it comes to designing and creating. There may be items and ideas mentioned here that are new to you; I hope they will make your beading more efficient and enjoyable. Additional tools, stringing supplies, and gluing products are described in the Appendix.

LIGHTING AND VIEWING SOLUTIONS

Your work area has modest requirements: good lighting, a level table surface, and a comfortable chair. If you want the help of a magnifying glass while you are working, you might consider one that has an optional light. You will find styles that clamp to a table, sit on the table, attach to floor stands, or are worn like a visor. Check stores that carry office supplies, electronics, sewing machines, beading supplies, and stitchery supplies for various models of magnifiers and lights.

MagEye's dual-lens magnifier is a lightweight spring headband that is worn like a visor. It is designed so the lenses are easily interchanged and flip out of the way when not in use. The 2.5X lens focuses at about 22″ and can even be worn with bifocals. The 4X lens is for work that is 12″ to 18″ away and thus is suitable for use at the sewing machine. It is so lightweight you can easily forget you're wearing it.

The Beam & Read light and magnifier hangs from your neck and has an adjustable light (the three Fresnel magnifiers can be used with or without the light). While convenient for home use, this compact light is especially useful for beading in the car or in a plane; also, you can mount it on your sewing machine by tying the strap to the machine's carrying handle and then hanging the magnifier in the front or back.

◄ These lighting and viewing solutions include MagEye's visor style with repositionable lens; the Enlarger-Lite (1+6) by SeldenCRAFT, mounted on a cast-iron base; and the Beam & Read magnifier with light, which can hang on a strap around the neck.

JEWELRY FINDINGS

All the metal rings, clasps, pin backs, and other hardware used to make jewelry are collectively called *findings*. Bead stores and craft stores stock several sizes and styles of most of the basic kinds of findings. It would be nice if we could open our box of jewelry findings every time we start a project and miraculously find the perfect rings and fasteners—or just pop into the local bead shop at midnight, when we are ready to attach the findings to finish off the piece.

The reality is that, with time, you will eventually accumulate a basic stock of findings that will serve you well in times of inspiration. Note that a piece of out-of-date jewelry is a perfect candidate for recycling, and its parts can resurface in a variety of wonderful new pieces. Be on the lookout for findings—and things that can act as findings. For example, the next time you are in a sporting goods store, look carefully through the fishing swivels and rings. You may find hardware for attaching multiple strands or clusters of beads in a unique way or for putting together beaded leashes or straps.

Most findings are available in base metals with a goldtone or silvertone finish. Many of the basic findings are also available in sterling silver, gold-filled, and karat gold. The jewelry projects in this book require simple assembly techniques. The necklace and earring strands are typically stitched to a jump ring. The ring is opened slightly when connecting the beaded piece to a necklace clasp or earring finding for pierced or clip-on earrings. If you need additional information about using findings (the options are numerous) as you get more involved with jewelry making, consult the References in this book or visit your local bead shop for some specific instruction.

For an added twist, consider painting jewelry findings so they play a part in the design instead of just having the traditional gold or silver finish. Paint It Pretty pens by Polychem Corporation were designed specially for use on metal finishes. The acrylic paint in these pens, which dries quickly and is permanent, comes in 24 colors, including opaques, pearls, metallics, and transparents (which allow the metal luster to shine through). Painting the flat end of head pins is a simple way to add a color accent to earrings. The fiber-tipped pens Paint It Pretty pens can also be used on plastic beads.

TIP: Use a bright color to paint the twisted ends of flex needles so they are easier to spot.

Attaching jewelry findings to the ends of beaded strands is an essential finishing touch for some projects. It is an integral part of the design and not a quick finish. This doesn't necessarily mean using an elaborate clasp or finding to finish a project, but it does mean using one that coordinates with the style of the jewelry and is attached securely. You are constructing pieces that may be around for generations, and you want to make sure they last over time.

Part 2
GET SET

Now that you have the basics down, it's time to gear up for the actual beading. This second part of the book helps you answer three important questions: How do I decide what to bead? What special materials do I need to do beading by machine? How do I set up my machine so I can use it to bead?

Chapter 3 focuses on planning and designing your project. You'll find guidance about color schemes, patterns, and design placement, as well as information about care of machine-beaded garments. As for any project, planning for machine beading is an important step toward achieving a beautiful and satisfying finished product.

Chapter 4 gets down to the nuts and bolts of beading by machine, and you'll probably find yourself referring to this chapter often as you proceed with the projects and beyond. With descriptions of helpful tools and appropriate thread choices, as well as detailed information about hoops, stabilizers, and transfer methods (including two easy-to-read tables), this chapter will become a well-thumbed reference as you explore the world of machine beading. The final section of this chapter takes you through the basic machine setup and general step-by-step procedures for beading by machine. At that point, you'll be all set to bead!

Chapter 3

•••••••••••

PLANNING YOUR PROJECT

When contemplating a beading project, think of this chapter as your supply basket. This basket contains the information and considerations required for almost any beadwork project. As the ideas start churning, this overview will guide you as you go about planning your project.

In these busy times, beading is an art that provides a simple avenue for creativity. It requires hardly more than beads and stringing supplies. Imagine a beaded ornament, a brooch, or a necklace incorporating new beads with those left over from a broken necklace from a cherished relative. It is a keepsake reminding us that our past influences our future. Because of all the design options you have, anything you bead becomes a unique reflection of you and will be a link to you for its lifetime.

BEAD WHAT?

When I hear that someone does beading by machine, I immediately picture beads being attached individually to highlight embroidery or enhance a fabric print. I should know better! There is so much more to beadwork by machine, and the possibilities are endless when you vary supplies and change bead styles and colors. If you are like me, you will want to learn the ins and outs of a technique before making your own innovations. After I master a basic technique, I try it backward, upside down, and in repetition, and sometimes I just use a portion of the basic steps. Try experimenting in this way—you too might have fun *not* following directions, and as a bonus, you may come up with a new twist to call your own.

When you are ready to begin, select a project that suits your tastes, time, and ambition so you will feel pleased with the process and the results. An easy way to begin working with beads is to attach beaded strands to fabric using a

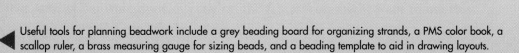

◀ Useful tools for planning beadwork include a grey beading board for organizing strands, a PMS color book, a scallop ruler, a brass measuring gauge for sizing beads, and a beading template to aid in drawing layouts.

idea for large beaded areas, even if other smaller areas with details are done directly on the garment, because it is easiest to do a minimum of beading directly on the garment.

Mark the main design areas on the garment with chalk, with washout pen, or with long basting stitches. Try on the garment to see how the design is affected by the waistline, by sleeves overlapping the front, and especially by the bustline (Figure 3.2). The placement and composition of the design may look good on the flat garment, but it may be unsatisfactory when you put it on. For example, a short-waisted person doesn't have much distance from shoulder to waist to accommodate a long design.

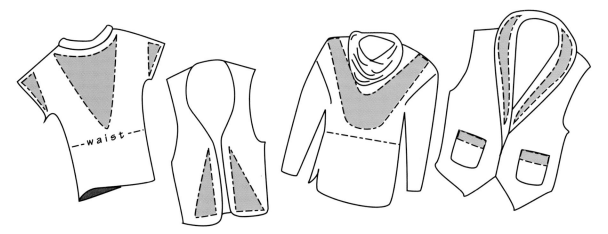

Figure 3.2 There are many options when you are considering where to add beadwork to a garment. For example, beadwork can be used to add accents or fill in bold design areas.

Consider using plastic stencils as inspiration for beading patterns. Used for quilting patterns and stencil painting, they offer many design opportunities. Areas in the design can be painted, appliquéd, or beaded by machine. Combinations of these techniques can produce effective results. Some stencil patterns are ideal for borders, while others, such as those designed for filling a quilt square, are perfect for the front of a garment. You may even find some designed specifically for necklines.

To achieve a versatile design, think of it as a grouping of sections or units, each of which can be pivoted or moved to suit your needs (Figure 3.3). Sometimes removing one section is the only change needed to simplify or shorten the design. Using reversed images of the pattern is an easy way to keep the integrity of the original design without having to create patterns from scratch.

When evaluating a potential design, consider the following questions:

Is the focal point in a pleasing area?
If you wear something (jacket, coat, vest, scarf) over the beaded garment, will the correct portion of the pattern be showing?
Does the layout accommodate the length and style of your hair?

Ready-to-wear garments like this denim blouse provide many areas for beaded embellishment. A stencil pattern by StenSource was used for inspiration and was traced on with a washout pen.

Figure 3.3 Plastic stencils make great beading patterns. This stencil by StenSource International is a garland of leaves and flowers. The dotted lines show it divided into units, which can be repeated, deleted, or mirrored to create new patterns. The matching heart stencil uses the same motifs.

Chapter 4

SUPPLIES FOR MACHINE BEADING & GENERAL MACHINE SETUP

Detail, details. Before discussing general sewing machine setup for beading, this chapter details important items to put into your supply basket as you prepare to bead by machine. Here you will find the technical information you need to know, including information on an assortment of tools and machine embroidery supplies. The beading isn't difficult once you have the necessary supplies on hand and understand when to use them. Some of this information for beading by machine could put a whole new twist on hand beading; for example, the use of transfer methods and some stabilizers could be helpful for hand beading projects. I have included in this chapter some innovative techniques using common and not-so-common supplies (refer to the Appendix for further information on supplies). Many of the techniques are my original ideas; those that are not are credited to the designers named.

◀ Here are some of the tools that are particularly useful for machine beading. Shown counterclockwise from left to right are specialty presser feet by Creative Feet, bent-nose tweezers, spring hoops, a wooden hoop, transfer pens, embroidery thread, and hemostats.

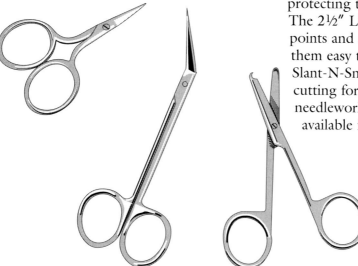

protecting the underlying canvas or fabric. The 2½″ Lit'l Snip features short, sharp points and oversized finger holes that make them easy to use for fine snipping. The 4½″ Slant-N-Snip has a slanted blade for precision cutting for paper cutwork and various needlework needs. These three styles are available from Dreamworks and Clotilde.

Figure 4.2 Shown from left to right, the Lit'l Snip, Slant-N-Snip, and Lift-N-Snip are unusual embroidery scissors that make snipping threads close to the work easy and precise.

Sewing Machine Needles

The size and type of the sewing machine needle must be compatible with the weight of the thread, the type of fabric, and size of the bead hole. A universal needle is good for most fabrics. A ballpoint is best for knit fabrics. The size #70-10 needle is the size used for most garment construction and is good for nearly all beading. Size #80-12 is bigger and also has a larger eye for heavier threads and ease of threading. Size #60-8 is sometimes needed for seed beads with smaller or irregular holes.

To make threading a machine needle easier, cut the thread at a slight angle. Place a white business card behind the needle so you can see the eye (some presser feet or their shanks have a white section for this purpose). Wet your index finger and rub it on the back side of the eye. The moisture will fill the hole and will draw the thread into it when you thread the needle.

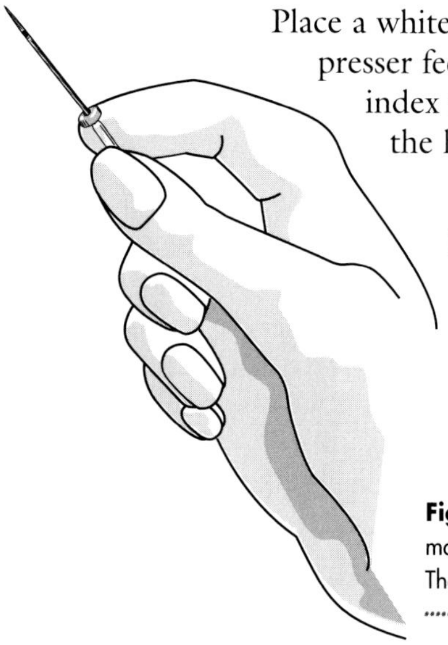

As a precaution, slide every bead onto a spare machine needle before sewing (Figure 4.3).With experience, you will be able to judge which beads will have an easy fit just by looking at the size of the hole in the bead. (Note that the size of the bead is not important—what counts is the size of the hole.) You can poke a machine needle into the plastic bag of seed beads and then into a bead to "try one on for size" before opening the bag.

Figure 4.3 To make sure the beads are the correct size for attaching individually with machine stitching, try each one on a needle which is the same size as the one in the machine. The bead should slide up to the large part of the needle.

Specialty Presser Feet

Most beading will be done without a presser foot on the machine, unless you're working with prestrung beads and sequins. For prestrung beads and sequins, use any foot with a deep groove on the underside where the beads can

WAT

Aqua
Wate
to fa
lace.
more
terns
Shar
make
mark

½" a
ironi
iron
or m

very
wove
can b
stitch
watei

LIQU

stabil
past i
(abou
the se
heat i
dissol

squee
porou
air-di
dry ir
you v
Use v
finish

and r
a dry

HOO

from
band

pass through smoothly. Creative Feet makes specialty press-er feet designed for this kind of work and made for use on all machines (Figure 4.4). Some machines have a cording or piping foot that will also work. If you can't find one made for your machine, ask your machine dealer about using an adapter so you can use feet from another brand.

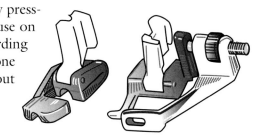

Figure 4.4 Specialty feet make couching beads and sequins quick and fun. On the left is shown the Pearls 'N Piping foot and on the right, the adjustable Sequins 'N Ribbon foot, both by Creative Feet.

The Sequins 'N Ribbon foot by Creative Feet has a ¼" slot on top for guiding the sequins strand or ribbons. You need a 6mm-wide stitch to sew across a standard-size sequin. (For more on attaching sequins, see Chapter 5.) Creative Feet also makes an accessory pair with ⅛" and ⅜" slots for guiding narrow widths. Set your stitch width to sew over the sequins.

Stabilizers and Hoops

Stabilizers and hoops are an important consideration when preparing your fabric for machine beading and any type of machine stitchery. When done properly, the finished piece lays flat, void of puckering, and thus nicely shows off the beading and stitchery. Lighter-weight fabrics require using a hoop or stabilizer because they tend to pucker easily, while heavier background fabrics are more stable and need little help. Some stabilizers can be hooped with the background fabric; when this isn't possible, the stabilizer can be pinned in place until the stitching can hold it. Selecting the correct stabilizer and hoop for a particular sewing project is a matter of knowledge, not skill. Table 4.1 covers many of the sewing situations you'll encounter. The table coordinates fabric, stitching, transfer method, and hoop.

Table 4.1 *Coordinating Fabric, Stabilizer, Transfer Method, and Hoop*

FABRIC	STABILIZER	TRANSFER METHOD	HOOP
Lightweight woven	Liquid stabilizer solution or Perfect Sew	Washout pen on fabric	5" or 7" spring hoop optional
Lightweight woven	None or lightweight tear-away	Washout pen on fabric	Wooden hoop
Medium-weight woven	None or lightweight tear-away	Washout pen on fabric	Wooden hoop
Medium-weight woven	Liquid stabilizer solution or Perfect Sew	Washout pen on fabric	5" or 7" spring hoop optional
Heavyweight (denim)	None needed	Permanent pen, washout pencil, or Sulky Transfer Pen on water-soluble stabilizer	7" spring hoop 8" or 10" wooden hoop
Sweatshirt fleece	Reynolds freezer paper or iron-on tear-away product	Permanent pen, washout pencil, or Sulky Transfer Pen on water-soluble stabilizer	None needed with freezer paper; 5" or 7" spring hoop or 8" wooden hoop with tear-away products
Single knit, sweater knit	Do Sew or Trace-A-Pattern	Permanent pen, washout pencil, or Sulky Transfer Pen on water-soluble stabilizer	5" or 7" spring hoop

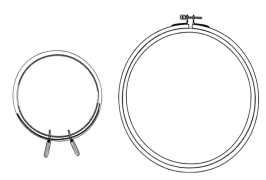

Figure 4.5 A spring hoop (left) is a plastic ring with a metal inner ring that springs open to hold the fabric in tension. The wooden hoop shown on the right is made specifically for machine embroidery; it has sturdy hardware so it can be tightened to hold the fabric very taut and also has a thin profile for easy insertion under the machine needle.

slotted screw allow me to pull the fabric extremely taut and to tighten the screw with a screw driver. The inexpensive craft hoops don't maintain good tension for machine embroidery and are awkward to use because of their wider bands. To prevent fabric from slipping in the hoop, wrap the inner ring with a ¾″ twill tape or nylon stay tape. Barely overlap the wraps to prevent adding bulk. Hand-stitch the end of the tape to itself on the edge of the ring to keep even tension against the outer ring.

I prefer to use spring hoops when working with medium- to heavyweight woven fabrics and with knits. A spring hoop coupled with the appropriate stabilizer produces a quality of stitching that is near perfection. A 5″ spring hoop fits comfortably in your hands and permits smooth movement for controlled stitching. A 7″ hoop accommodates a larger embroidery area but is more difficult to maneuver within the open area of the sewing machine. The inner, metal ring of the 5″ and 7″ spring hoops can be wrapped with Dermicel, a ½″-wide rayon hypoallergenic medical tape, to minimize the loosening of the fabric in the hoop. This tape is adhesive-backed, so rub a talcum powder on the wrapped hoop to absorb the excessive stickiness before using it.

Consider using 2″, 3″, or 4″ spring hoops when the area on a garment is difficult to fit into a larger hoop. Sometimes tricky areas on necklines and shoulder seams require a smaller hoop. The smaller hoops can be used to avoid hooping over beaded areas. The smaller the hoop, the better the tension on the fabric. Smaller sizes are handy when signing your work because of the ease of movement while stitching details.

THREAD CHOICES

Most of the time, in the machine needle, you will want to use clear monofilament thread or thread that is the same color as the background fabric, so the stitches won't show. When working on a piece that includes machine embroidery, you can attach beads using the same embroidery thread. Even though rayon is not a strong thread (#40 is standard weight for machine embroidery), I have never lost beads attached with it, even on garments that are machine-washed (turned inside out).

Machine stitchery on fabric is usually tied off by taking four to five tiny stitches at the beginning and end of each motif or when changing colors. This method of locking the stitches is secure through countless machine washings and wear. Some of the beading projects in this book require that the stitching be secured by tying a couple of square knots or granny knots and sealing them with a sealant like Fray Check or one of the glues suggested in the Appendix (Unique Stitch is good because it dries with a rubber-like finish and thus isn't irritating to the skin). One drop of sealant is enough for at least ten knots, so apply a small amount to the knot with the tip of a straight pin. Craft glues that are permanent and flexible will also work. The easiest product to use straight from the container is G-S Hypo-Tube cement because of the pinpoint applicator tip on the tube and the ability of the glue to saturate the knot.

The list that follows presents the choices you have when determining what thread to use in the needle of the sewing machine. (If you are feeling innovative, be sure to check out the Appendix listing of other natural, synthetic, and metal supplies that can be used for stringing beads to be couched by machine.) Note that thread deliberately exposed when stitching between beads can become an integral part of the design. Metallic threads, colored elastics, and cord and braids are good choices when you use this technique.

- *Polyester machine embroidery thread* is good for machine-stitched jewelry because of its strength and fine (#40) weight. This is finer than the thread used for garment construction. Neon, a polyester embroidery thread, is made by Madeira. Pfaff and New Home also distribute strong synthetic embroidery threads. Although cotton-wrapped polyester thread may also work, this all-purpose sewing thread will produce stitching that is coarse because of the thread's heavier weight.
- *Nymo nylon thread,* the next best option after silk, is available in a few basic colors (see the Resources section of this book). Nymo is very fine and can be used for stringing beads or in the machine.
- *Monofilament* comes in clear and smoke color. Machine embroidery suppliers carry the lightest weight (.004). Monofilament is strong and can take the heat of an iron. When using beads with very small holes, you will need to use monofilament with a #60-8 needle and might only be able to take one stitch to attach each bead.

Bobbin thread for machine embroidery may be cotton, polyester, or nylon lingerie thread. All of these are the same light weight as rayon or metallic thread used in the needle. The top and bobbin threads should be of similar weight when possible to produce the best results. Cotton bobbin thread is preferred by most professionals. If your machine beading is dimensional or will be seen on both sides, as in the Beaded Richelieu or jewelry projects later in this book, use a bobbin wound with the same thread as you use on top.

TRANSFER METHODS

Washout pens and pencils have been a basic method of safely marking fabric for sewing projects for as long as I can remember. Air pens have a purple or sometimes pink ink that disappears from the fabric in a few minutes (the actual time depends on the humidity in the air).

Table 4.2 presents the use of various transfer methods. Some are permanent, while others will wear or wash away. Different types of fabric and backgrounds are listed so you can determine which combinations work best.

Table 4.2 *Transfer Methods for Various Fabrics*

FABRIC	PEN	PENCIL	OTHER METHOD
Water-soluble stabilizer	Pigma, Sharpie, washout pen, Sulky Transfer Pen	Clotilde's washout pencil	Permanent fine-tip artist's pens, Clotilde's washable transfer paper
Light-colored fabrics	Washout pen, air pen	Pounce (see Resources)	
Dark-colored fabrics	—	Clotilde's washout pencil	Clotilde's washable transfer paper
Washable napped fabric (terry cloth, corduroy)	—	—	Draw pattern on water-soluble stabilizer instead of fabric and hoop on top
Nonwashable fabrics (velvet, satin, woolens)	—	—	Draw pattern with Pigma or Sharpie pen on heat-reactive stabilizer
Tulle, netting	—	—	Draw pattern on water-soluble stabilizer and use spring hoop
Sheers (organdy, chiffon, batiste)	Washout pen, air pen, Pigma, Sharpie	—	Draw pattern on water-soluble stabilizer with washout pencil and use wooden or spring hoop
Ultrasuede	—	Washable pencil	Sulky Transfer Pen on paper, then iron on Ultrasuede
Prints	Washout pen, Pigma	—	Pounce, Sulky Transfer Pen on paper, then iron on fabric
Knits (single, sweater)	—	—	Draw pattern on water-soluble stabilizer instead of knit and use spring hoop
Sweatshirt fleece, denim	—	—	Draw pattern backward on freezer paper and iron on wrong side *or* draw pattern on water-soluble stabilizer and use spring hoop

GENERAL SEWING MACHINE SETUP

Beading with a sewing machine starts with the same machine settings as if you were going to do machine embroidery. To help keep troubleshooting to a minimum, use the numbered directions that follow as a reference until the procedure becomes second nature. Seek out a machine embroidery instructor before talking to a sewing machine repairman about changing the machine settings. Teachers will assure you that changing machine tensions is OK and will not throw off the settings. The machine's top tension was designed to be changed when sewing different types and thicknesses of fabrics. The bobbin tension is usually adjustable, but not all machines allow access to do so—refer to your machine's manual. Attach an extension table to the machine if it doesn't set into a sewing table (see the beginning of this chapter for directions on how to make your own extension table).

1. Remove the presser foot, the shank it attaches to, and the screw securing the shank to the machine. Put them in a container for safekeeping. (A Bernina presser foot incorporates the shank with the foot and has a lever instead of a screw.)

2. Insert a #70-10 universal or ballpoint machine needle.

3. Thread the machine with the appropriate thread as suggested for your project or in this chapter. Insert a bobbin wound with an appropriate thread as suggested for the project.

4. Lower the feed dogs. If your machine cannot do this, you might have an accessory plate that covers the feed dogs. These are usually cumbersome when using a hoop, but you can make a better-suited one from a 2″ square cut from an index card. Cut a slot in the middle that is the same size as the one on the machine's throat plate so the needle can straight-stitch or zigzag without sewing into the card. To do this, poke the closed blade of embroidery scissors through the card. Tape the card to the throat plate.

5. As in free-motion embroidery, set the width on 0 and the length on 0. When you want to sew over a strand of beads, make sure the zigzag is set wide enough to clear the beads and set at about a 3 length if using a foot. If the stitch is too wide, it will tunnel or draw up the fabric.

6. Lower the presser bar. Even though you aren't using a presser foot on the machine, it is important to engage the top tension.

7. Generally, the top tension for machine embroidery should be a little looser than normal, so set the top tension one notch lower than normal. (In most cases this is close to the proper setting for machine embroidery, but it will vary with different machines.) On the wrong side of the fabric, you should see the top and bobbin thread on every stitch.

8. Usually the bobbin tension is slightly tighter than normal. You may have to tighten the bobbin tension if it persists in pulling to the right side of the fabric. If the bobbin case has two screws, tighten the one closest to the opening where the thread comes out by turning it to the right. Do this over a counter in case the screw falls out. The other screw fastens the tension spring to the bobbin case. Correct tension for any thread is achieved when the bobbin inserted into the bobbin case, suspended as you hold onto the thread tail, drops only when the thread is yanked. The bobbin case should drop slowly, then stop (like a spider on the string of a web).

9. Hoop a scrap of fabric (and stabilizer if you are using one). Sew a running stitch, which is a "straight stitch" that may curve, circle, sketch, or roam anywhere on the fabric. You are in control and the stitch flows from the needle like ink from a pen. Look at the stitching on both sides of the fabric and adjust the tensions as needed so that you see *only the top thread* on the right side of the fabric.

10. As mentioned earlier in this chapter under "Thread Choices," it is important to secure the top and bobbin threads at the beginning of the beadwork. Most of the time it is sufficient to take several short stitches to secure the thread to the fabric before starting to bead. Here is

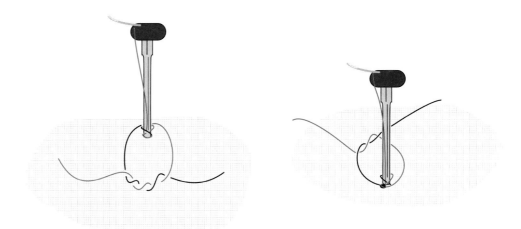

Figure 4.6 This is a method for tying a surgeon's knot around the machine needle at the start of machine stitching to secure the top and bobbin threads together.

another method of securing threads at the beginning: Turn the handwheel until the tip of the needle is lowered into the fabric so the eye doesn't show. Wrap the top and bobbin threads in opposite directions around the machine needle and tie two surgeon's knots around the needle (Figure 4.6). You can apply a speck of Fray Check on the knot using the tip of a straight pin. Proceed with the stitching and cover the knot with beadwork.

Now that you are familiar with these basic procedures, let's do some beading!

Part 3
············
LET'S BEAD!

Welcome to the unique world of beading with a sewing machine. You will find techniques ranging from the expected (embellishing printed fabrics) to the unexpected (making beaded note cards). We will be capitalizing on the sewing machine's tension adjustments on top and in the bobbin, which allow for a variety of threads, yarns, and ribbons to be used with machine stitching. Beadwork by machine takes practice and precision, just like learning to write your name; however, you may be surprised at the kinds of projects you can accomplish just with beginner's skills.

The projects for beading by machine are categorized according to the primary techniques they use. In this part of the book you will find projects using couching techniques, techniques for attaching beads individually, ways to finish edges and create fringes, bead embroidery techniques, and serger applications for machine beading.

Initially, even avid sewing enthusiasts might think that they can bead faster by hand than by machine—until they try it. Beading by machine may be a little slow in the beginning, but with a little practice, the speed and rhythm pick up. I like both processes—hand beading and beading by machine—but I find a mechanical advantage when relying on the sewing machine's tension. When the work is properly stabilized and hooped, the finished beading is strong and is stitched with the precision of very fine handwork. When beading by machine, it is best to anchor all the stitching at the beginning and ending (see Chapter 4) and snip threads as you go (keeping the work area clean of thread tails is easier than having to tie them off by hand later).

The projects in this book utilize basic skills so that all stitchers can achieve success. An unusual use of supplies combined with a novel approach to beading provides you with many interesting projects. I hope that you will be inspired to experiment with threads and patterns to create your own versions of the simple ideas that I present.

Chapter 5

••••••••••

COUCHING BEAD STRANDS

Couching is a technique in which strung beads are attached by stitching over the prestrung strand rather than sewing through each bead hole individually. When using the technique of couching to apply beading to fabric you have the choice of either using special presser feet or using no presser feet at all (for doing free-motion embroidery). There are advantages to and tricks for accomplishing both methods.

There are two ways of working with beads that you string yourself. One way is to stitch over the strand of prestrung beads to fill areas solid with beading. The other way is to sew over the strand, isolating groups of beads, as done on the Tapestry Eyeglass Case in Chapter 8. Either way, you can choose to string the beads ahead of time (especially if you're using all the same color) or else to string them at the sewing machine while the work is in progress. The latter approach will give you more flexibility so you can decide on colors and sizes just as you need them. I can understand how this spontaneous approach might be unsettling, but it is a good exercise in designing by instinct. Sometimes we bury ourselves in overplanning and forget to enjoy the adventure!

PRESTRUNG BEADS AND SEQUINS

There are three types of prestrung beads: molded (or permanently glued) on the strand, prestrung and movable on the strand, and cross-locked (Figure 5.1). The timesaving feature of using inexpensive prestrung plastic craft beads is ideal for costumes or other novelty wear, and they are readily available in craft and fabric stores. Such beads are usually available in 2mm to 4mm sizes. Be aware that the quality of the paint varies on these plastic beads.

Prestrung beads can be couched using a presser foot with a wide, deep groove on the underside. Presser feet such as this are known as piping or cording feet, and the beads will pass smoothly under this type of foot during stitching. Creative Feet manufactures specialty feet in a few different styles which are designed to sew on beads, sequins, ribbon, and elastic (see Resources). For additional information on sewing machine feet, consult Chapter 4.

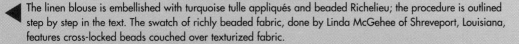

◄ The linen blouse is embellished with turquoise tulle appliqués and beaded Richelieu; the procedure is outlined step by step in the text. The swatch of richly beaded fabric, done by Linda McGehee of Shreveport, Louisiana, features cross-locked beads couched over texturized fabric.

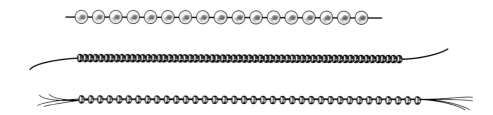

Figure 5.1 The types of prestrung beads shown here are plastic beads molded to a strand, individually strung beads, and glass cross-locked beads.

Figure 5.2 Stitching over a molded bead strand can be done with ease using a Pearls 'N Piping foot (by Creative Feet) or a cording foot whose groove on the underside glides smoothly over the beads. If you can hoop the fabric, you can carefully free-motion stitch over the strand without any foot for greater mobility.

Set the machine for a zigzag wide enough to clear the beads (Figure 5.2). This setting would be 4mm to 6mm or the widest setting on older machines. If the stitch is too wide it will tunnel or draw the fabric up around the bead (and the stitches will show). The stitch length is about the same setting. You will see that the stitching rolls over the beads, falling in the spaces between. Before threading the machine, insert the beaded strand under the foot and lower the presser bar. Turning the handwheel manually, take a few stitches, checking to see if the zigzag setting is wide enough. It should just clear the bead on either side. The richly beaded swatch in the photograph at the beginning of this chapter was stitched using this method. Imagine a vest or a purse decorated this way!

To couch over a strand of beads that have been strung by hand, secure the beginning of the string by stitching *over* the strand by the knotted end (Figure 5.3a). Pull the knot snug to the zigzag. Cover the knot by flipping the strand over it and stitching (couching) it in place (Figure 5.3b). When the beading is finished, the thread tail is secured by threading it to the underside with a hand sewing needle and taking a few stitches to tie off. You can also tie it around the strand with a single knot at a few spots between the beads before tying it off on the back (Figure 5.4).

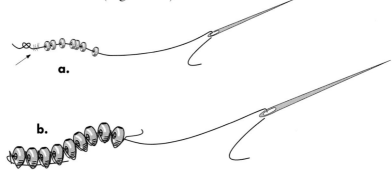

Figure 5.3 Anchor a strand of beads by stitching over it near the knotted end. When you start to stitch over the beads, catch the thread tail underneath the strand. With this method, you can string any color or number of beads as they are needed.

Figure 5.4 This is the method for tying off the thread tail at the end of a length of hand-strung beads.

Figure 5.5 It is possible to couch a prestrung strand of beads on the edge of a hem with a Pearls 'N Piping foot and a zigzag stitch wide enough to clear the beads. The stitches will fall in between the beads and will seem to disappear.

With this setup, you can attach bead strands on top of fabric or else on the edge with only the left side of the zigzag stitch sewn to the fabric. The right side of the stitch wraps around the strand when stitching "in the air" (Figure 5.5). Usually the top and bobbin threads match the fabric, but you can take this opportunity to have fun with novelty threads like metallics and multicolors to show off the unique stitching pattern that occurs.

Cross-locked Beads

Cross-locked beads are glass seed beads that are strung (not glued) on four interwoven threads that keep them locked in place and evenly spaced. This braiding prevents the beads from twisting and turning while being applied. The round-style beads are available in many colors slightly larger than size 11/0 (11°) and also in a black faceted style. The faceted beads are eye-catching, but they may snag fabric and are more difficult to apply since the beads drag against the foot.

Use needle size #80-10 and a cording foot or Pearls 'N Piping foot by Creative Feet. Test a medium zigzag of about 2.5mm length and width on your machine to make sure it clears the bead. If you break a bead, pick up the fragments and check the needle for damage. A needle with a bad tip will tear fabric and shred the top thread while stitching. If the needle breaks or needs to be replaced, insert a new one and take five short stitches to secure the thread tails. The space left by a broken bead can be filled by sewing an intersecting line of beads or attaching a single bead later. Clean your machine thoroughly, removing any glass fragments.

At the beginning and end of a design, pull or break beads off the thread chain, clearing about 1½″ of thread tails. For breaking beads, Nancy Zieman, author and sewing show host, suggests using a modified pair of needle-nose pliers to prevent the broken glass from cutting the braid. Tape a large paper clip to the top surface of one of the jaws to make a temporary spacer. This will prevent the pliers from closing completely. Note that it is a good idea to wear safety glasses while breaking beads.

Once you have cleared the thread tails, tie an overhand knot next to the beginning bead and the ending bead. Sew the thread tail into a seam or secure it to the fabric with stitching (Figure 5.6a). You can also stitch this tail to the fabric and then sew the beads over it at the beginning (Figure 5.6b). At the end of the design, tuck the thread tails under the beads and stitch over them to secure.

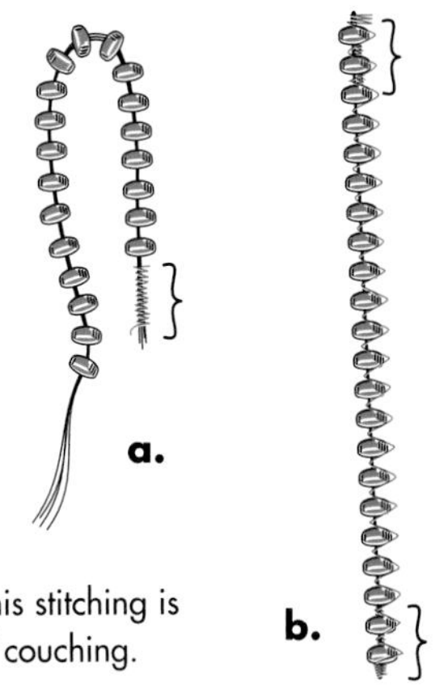

a.

b.

Figure 5.6 The beginning of a strand of cross-locked beads is anchored by stitching over the thread tails. This stitching is covered with the strand and the ending tail is tucked under the strand so it can be anchored in the last ½″ of couching.

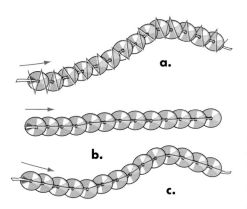

Figure 5.7 Sequins on a strand can be stitched with a straight stitch that is the right length so the needle only goes in the sequin hole. A zigzag stitch can be used if it is wide enough to clear the sequins. A Sequins 'N Ribbon foot guides the strand smoothly.

Prestrung Sequins

Prestrung sequins can be couched in place using an appliqué foot since it has a groove wide enough for most widths to pass through. Use monofilament thread on top and use bobbin thread to match the fabric. The Sequins 'N Ribbon foot by Creative Feet has a ¼″ slot on top designed for this job. An accessory pair of Creative Feet have ⅛″ and ⅜″ slots for couching sequins, ribbon, elastic, and trims. Set the stitch width at 6mm so the stitching will clear the sequins (Figure 5.7a). Sewing through the sequins will not break the needle, but it will ruin the tip quickly (remember that a ruined tip may damage the fabric). The stitch length is at least 3mm. (If your machine doesn't have a stitch wide enough, you can carefully sew down the center with a long straight stitch into the hole of each sequin, as shown in Figures 5.7b and 5.7c.)

Another method for attaching sequins is to use a blind hem stitch, which is *not* as visible as a zigzag since it doesn't cross the sequins as often. You can also attach sequins by sewing on one side of the sequins for a few stitches and then jumping over to sew on the other side for a few stitches (Figure 5.8). This is an automatic stitch for some machines and can be programmed into others. If you are skilled in machine embroidery, glue the string of sequins to the fabric (with glue stick), put on a darning foot, and use any of the above stitching patterns with free-motion movement. Pat Rodgers, who produced the video *Free Motion Machine Embroidery and Beading by Machine,* suggests yet another method for sewing sequins: Move the strand to the left while taking a few stitches on the opposite side and then move it to the right and take a few stitches on the other side. Continue stitching on alternating sides. (A darning foot may be helpful for this technique.)

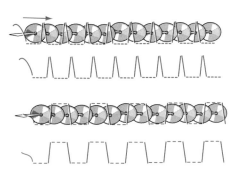

Figure 5.8 Use a blind hem stitch or program a variation when you want less thread to show as it crosses over the sequins.

CUSTOM-STRUNG STRANDS

Beads can be strung ahead of time in a specific or random order. If you want to transfer beads from a hank onto your stringing thread, either hold both strands together and tie an overhand knot or join the strands using a weaver's knot (see Chapter 2). Gently slide the beads off the cotton hank thread onto the stronger thread (Nymo #B or poly/cotton construction thread), easing them past the knot.

Another stringing method is to simply take one stitch and pull up the bobbin thread (this will be the stringing thread). Note: If you are using Nymo #B, wind it slowly on the bobbin to prevent stretching the thread (stretched thread can cause the stitching to pucker). When possible, try to match the color of the bobbin thread to the color of the background fabric. In the machine needle, use machine embroidery thread to match the fabric or use monofilament thread. Pull out about 20″ of bobbin thread so you will have an adequate length to work with. If you need more bobbin thread as you are working, take a few short stitches to secure the machine stitching. Thread the beading strand (bobbin thread) through a hand needle and take it to the back and secure with a few knots around the previous stitching. Remove your work from the machine and start again by pulling another length of bobbin thread up to be used for stringing. Depending on the size of the beads' holes, string the beads on the bobbin thread using a hand sewing needle, a beading needle, or another type of threader (threaders are described in Chapter 2).

Figure 5.9 For added texture, use a novelty thread for stringing the beads and anchor loops of it between beads.

If the holes in the beads are large enough and you want the stringing thread to be part of the design, you can use metallic yarns or cords like those from Kreinik, Madeira, and Sulky. Between beads, the cord can be stitched to the fabric in free-form designs or used to outline shapes or edges of appliqués (Figure 5.9). You can make a loop with the cord (with a bead or bauble in the middle of the loop) and create a loopy fringe as shown on my scarf in the Artists' Gallery at the back of the book.

Beaded Richelieu

Richelieu is a traditional hand embroidery technique where you make a bar of stitching that spans from one side of a cutwork opening to the other. It is decorative and also functions as a way to support the opening since fabric has been cut away. This is particularly important for large cutwork areas and curved openings. For example, a crescent shape will flap open if the fabric edges are not drawn together with Richelieu bars. When done by machine, the Richelieu bars are straight stitching covered with satin stitching.

Bette Blande, of San Diego, California, originated the idea of making beaded bars with a sewing machine instead of the traditional satin stitching. I have designed the pattern shown on the pink blouse on pages 46 and 51 by combining her idea with additional stitching techniques (Figure 5.10). The design includes veins made of prestrung beads. The Richelieu bars are strong and are snug to the edges of the cutwork. Notice that a subtle color appears within the embroidery design; I have used a single layer of turquoise tulle in the appliqués to produce this effect.

Figure 5.10 The pattern for the Beaded Richelieu project finishes approximately 4½″ × 8″. The shaded shapes represent the beaded Richelieu, and the shapes with grids are appliqués, each with a vein of beads on top.

SUPPLIES

  2mm prestrung faux pearls (approximately 112 beads or a 20″ length) on a double strand of poly/cotton thread to match fabric
  colored tulle to complement fabric
  rayon thread to match fabric
  water-soluble stabilizer, 12″ × 12″
  5″ spring hoop
  10″ wooden hoop

MACHINE SETUP

  Stitch length: 0
  Stitch width: 0
  Feed dogs: down or covered
  Presser foot: none

Upper tension: a little looser than normal
Lower tension: normal
Needle: #70-10
Top thread: rayon to match fabric
Bobbin thread: rayon to match fabric

1. Draw the embroidery pattern on water-soluble stabilizer with a washout pen (or pencil) or a Pigma pen whose color is similar to the fabric color. On the fabric, use the washout pen to draw the cutting line for the neckline and shoulder seam. Do not cut on these lines yet, but allow extra fabric so there will be enough for the hoop to grasp.

2. Center and pin the water-soluble stabilizer with the pattern on the wrong side of the fabric. On the right side of the fabric, pin a single layer of tulle over the design area. Transfer all the straight pins to the wrong side of the fabric. Place a section of the design in a 5″ spring hoop, with the pattern facing up. This size hoop will keep the fabric in sufficient tension and is easy to move as the work progresses.

3. Straight-stitch around the 12 appliqué shapes three times (Figure 5.11). Stitch each one all three times before moving to the next. These rows will pad the satin stitching that you will do later. Trim all the thread tails on the top and the bottom, close to the stitching. With the fabric still hooped, trim the excess tulle close to the stitching with your best embroidery scissors. Re-hoop as needed so the fabric is easier to trim. Use tweezers or hemostats to grip the tulle when trimming hard-to-reach areas.

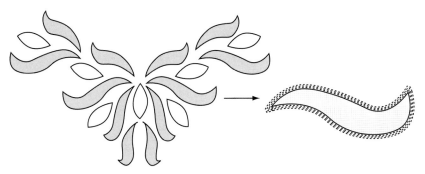

Figure 5.11 The shaded areas are the 12 appliqué shapes that are each stitched three times around the perimeter.

4. Hoop the fabric with the stabilizer side facing up. Straight-stitch around the seven cutwork openings three times each (Figure 5.12). Mark the ends of each Richelieu bar with a washout pen on the right side of the fabric by holding the hooped fabric up to a light so you can see the original pattern lines.

5. Re-hoop the fabric in 10″ wooden hoop with the right side of the fabric facing up. Satin-

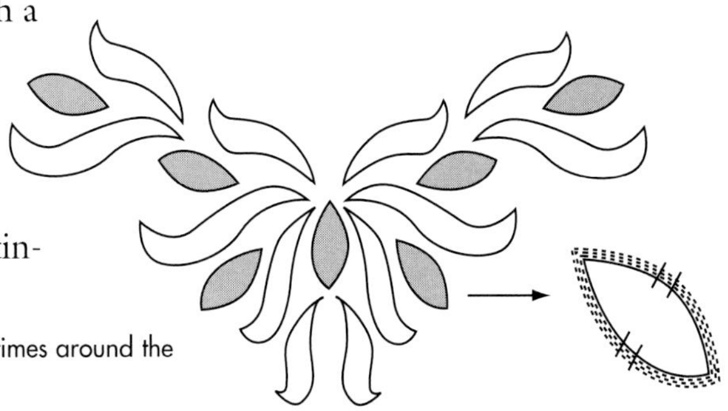

Figure 5.12 The highlighted cutwork shapes are also stitched three times around the perimeter. The lines mark where the beaded Richelieu bars will occur.

stitch each appliqué shape with a satin-stitch length and 1¾ width or a width just wide enough to cover all the straight stitching (Figure 5.13). A narrow width is the goal. Within the seven cutwork shapes, carefully cut away the fabric and stabilizer next to the stitching. Precision cutting now will be rewarded with perfect edges later.

Figure 5.13 Satin-stitch over the original three rows of straight stitching on the 12 appliqué shapes.

6. *Richelieu bars:* If you follow my design exactly, you will find that five 2mm beads span the cutwork opening for each Richelieu bar, but actually you will need only four beads for each bar. If you use another cutwork pattern or different size of bead, plan to leave a 1mm gap shy of the cutwork width so the strand of beads can snug the opening and the beads won't interfere with the satin stitching to follow. To begin, thread a twisted flex needle, Big Eye Needle, or a hand sewing needle with a 2-yard length (to be used as a double strand) of poly/cotton construction thread the same color as the fabric.

7. String about 14″ of beads on the double strand (the double strand makes strong, rigid bars and is easily secured when stitched upon).

8. Take one stitch near the end of a cutwork opening to pull up the bobbin thread. Hold the double strand of poly/cotton on the stitched edge of the cutwork and stitch on it, moving toward one end of the first bar (Figure 5.14). Secure the strand again at the end of the first bar. Hold the double strand out of the way and move the hoop as you take about three stitches "in the air" while stitching across the cutwork opening. When you reach the mark at the opposite end of the bar, put the needle into the fabric and slide four beads on the double strand, across the opening. Make sure this is the correct amount and that the angle of the Richelieu bar is correct. Stitch *over* the double strand once. While the needle is in the fabric, pull the double strand to bring the cut edges closer and snug to the beads. Stitch through the double strand at the end of the bar. Continue stitching on it while working your way away from the bar toward the end of the next bar. Make the next Richelieu bar in the same way and finish by stitching on the double strand for about ⅜″. Trim the tails of the double strand.

9. Starting at one end of the opening, satin-stitch with a 1¾ width, covering the straight stitching and carefully avoiding the beads. You will need to

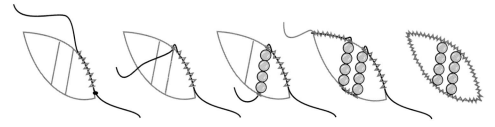

Figure 5.14 These are the six steps for making strong beaded Richelieu bars in cutwork. The beading strand is secured with a tiny zigzag and is anchored before and after each beaded Richelieu bar.

pivot the hoop slowly while stitching a smooth, even edge. Secure the stitching with five tiny straight stitches on the outside edge of the satin stitch.

10. When all the beaded Richelieu bars are finished, remove the work from the machine. Turn it over with the wrong side facing up. With tweezers, grip the thread (the one stitched "in the air") behind each beaded bar and carefully snip each end next to the satin stitching.

11. *Beaded veins:* Thread a flex needle, Big Eye Needle, or hand sewing needle with a 2-yard length of construction thread as done for the Richelieu bars. Take one stitch inside the satin stitching of an appliqué shape and pull up the bobbin thread. Hold on to a 3″ tail of the beading strand and stitch on it, securing it to the fabric (don't cut it yet) (Figure 5.15). String an even number of beads (8–12) for the first vein. Slide up two beads at a time and stitch over the strand to snug them in place. Repeat until the vein is finished, then work your way back to the starting point by stitching over the strand and the tail end after every bead. Cut the beading strand, leaving a 3″ tail.

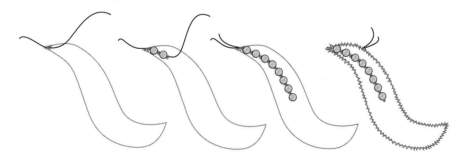

Figure 5.15 A strand of beads is couched for the vein, and the thread tails of the strand are secured later, under the satin stitching that goes around the appliqué shape.

12. With the work still in the machine, satin-stitch over the straight stitching and over the thread tails at the same time for about ¾″. Cut the strands and finish satin stitching around the appliqué shape. Secure the stitching with about five tiny straight stitches next to the outside of the satin stitching.

13. The water-soluble stabilizer may be torn from the outside of satin-stitched areas since it has been perforated by the stitching. Grip it with hemostats in hard-to-reach areas. Soak off the remaining water-soluble stabilizer in warm water.

Chapter 6
. . . .

ATTACHING BEADS & SEQUINS INDIVIDUALLY

The only limitations associated with attaching beads individually with the sewing machine are related to the size of the beads and the bead hole. Bead thickness is measured in the same direction as the hole. Most sewing machines cannot sew a bead thicker than ¼" (Figure 6.1). Anything thicker will not allow the needle bar to go all the way down to take a stitch. The other size limitation is the size of the hole in the bead, which has to be large enough for a threaded sewing machine needle to pass through. Note that while seed beads may appear to be all the same, the hole size is actually not consistent from bead to bead. Thus, it is extremely helpful to take a few minutes before starting a machine beaded project to try the beads on a spare machine needle. For your project, use only those beads which are able to slide all the way up the narrow length of the shaft.

Generally, seed beads can only be sewn on with one or two stitches because of they have such small holes. Whenever possible, use three to four stitches to attach beads with larger holes.

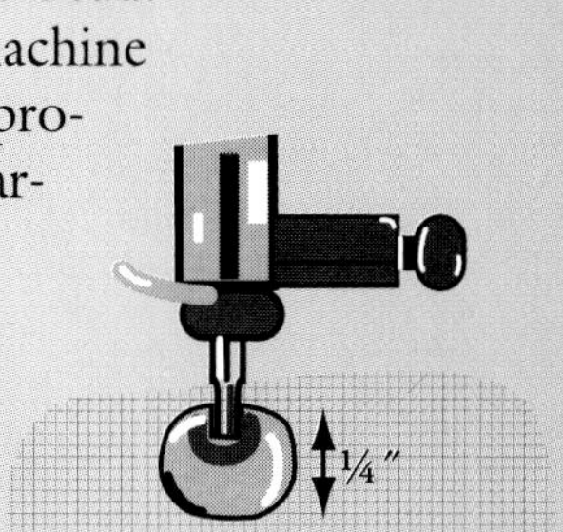

Figure 6.1 For most sewing machines, a bead or bead hole cannot be longer than ¼". This is the approximate distance between the needle bar and the throat plate when the needle is at its lowest point. This varies with machines.
....

A Button and Charm Necklace is a fun way to express yourself using treasures you have collected over time. The necklace pictured dangles a pair of "spare scissors" for good luck. Tassel earrings are such fun to make, you may want to whip up a pair for each of your favorite outfits. These multistrand necklaces use beads and buttons made from many different materials, including coconut, glass, and plastic.

General Instructions

MACHINE SETUP

Stitch length: 0
Stitch width: 0
Feed dogs: lowered or covered
Presser feet: none
Upper tension: normal
Lower tension: normal
Needle: #70-10 or #60-8 for smaller holes
Top thread: depends on project
Bobbin thread: depends on project
Hoop: 5″ or 7″ spring hoop

1. Start by taking a single stitch. Pull the bobbin thread to the top of the fabric by tugging on the needle's thread tail (Figure 6.2). When you first bring up a loop of the bobbin thread, pull on the side closest to you. This is the tail end of the bobbin thread. Pulling on the other side will just unwind the bobbin. While holding both thread tails in your left hand, take four small stitches to lock the stitching before starting to embroider or bead.

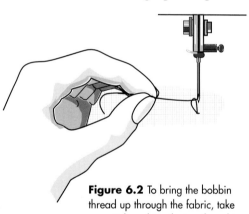

Figure 6.2 To bring the bobbin thread up through the fabric, take one stitch and tug the top thread to make a loop of bobbin thread. Pull on the part of the loop closest to you to retrieve the tail end of the bobbin.

2. With the needle in the raised position, hold the first bead in your left hand and slide it up the machine needle. Hold it against the needle with your left index finger while turning the handwheel until the needle barely punctures the fabric (Figure 6.3a). If your machine can take one stitch at a time, tap the foot control so the needle will continue down and finish in the raised position. If your machine cannot do this, turn the handwheel manually to complete the stitch. *Caution:* Until you gain complete confidence in your ability to sew safely without a presser foot on your machine, I suggest that you keep your foot on the foot control only when taking a stitch.

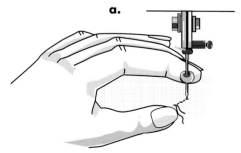

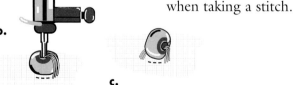

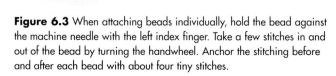

Figure 6.3 When attaching beads individually, hold the bead against the machine needle with the left index finger. Take a few stitches in and out of the bead by turning the handwheel. Anchor the stitching before and after each bead with about four tiny stitches.

With your fingers so close to the work, you don't want the machine to take a stitch until you are ready. I take my foot off the pedal even when threading the needle.

3. Move the work slightly and turn the handwheel so you will stitch on the side of the bead where you started. Repeat until you have attached the bead with two to five stitches (Figure 6.3b). The number of stitches depends on the size of the bead's hole. You will be able to tell when it is too tight for another stitch. Since your machine is set for balanced tension, the beads will be attached securely and will roll to one side so the hole is *not* facing up (Figure 6.3c). The bead cannot roll over if the stitching radiates from the hole, although this does produce a distinct decorative effect.

You can attach beads close together, in clusters (Figure 6.4a), with the securing stitches seeming almost invisible. When the color of the thread used through the needle blends with the background fabric, the beads appear sparse and seem to be sprinkled on the fabric (Figure 6.4b). To keep the thread continuous between beads that are widely spaced, you can doodle delicate designs or words on the fabric (Figure 6.4c). This also secures each bead individually. If you don't wish to use this effect, just take four or five short stitches before and after attaching each bead to lock them in place.

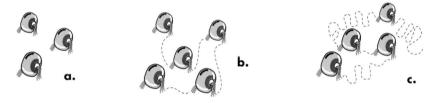

Figure 6.4 Beads can be attached individually, in clusters, or among doodling stitches. The stitches between the beads will secure the threads.

ATTACHING SEQUINS

Attaching sequins individually is a matter of stitching in and out of each hole a few times (Figure 6.5). As with any machine stitching, take a few small stitches at the beginning and the end to secure the threads. If you want the sequins in a particular layout, put glue stick on the back of an extra sequin and put it on the fabric, replacing one in the design. Repeat until the entire pattern is glued.

To overlap sequins, start with the one at the bottom. Stitch to secure it on both sides, then plant the needle on one side. Overlap the next sequin to the hole of the first one. Stitch into the hole and over to the other side. Repeat. For a variation, place a smaller sequin or a bead on top of the hole and sew through it at the same time you are stitching through the sequins.

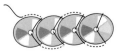

Figure 6.5 Sequins can be attached individually with two or more stitches that radiate from the hole. When attached in a sequence, the stitching goes from one side to the other, stitching in the center hole each time.

Beaded Silk Ribbon Pillow

This silk ribbon pillow showcases the kind of intricate detail that makes a project an instant heirloom.

Silk ribbons were used to create tiny dimensional flowers on the small lace pillow shown in the photograph above. A manufactured trim outlines the heart. The ribbon embroidery and beading were done with a sewing machine including the flower centers, ribbon border, and background of opalescent sequins. This keepsake has an inconspicuous heart-shaped pocket of English netting on the underside. My daughter and the tooth fairy are using it now, but it can become a ring pillow if I stitch two ribbons near the center.

YLI features silk ribbon with 185 colors in 4mm width, 85 in 2mm width, 76 in 7mm width, 33 in 13mm width, and 30 in 32mm width. The delicate, light-as-air quality of silk ribbon produces beautiful gathers and knots and can be used to create exquisite dimensional stitchery by hand and machine. The fine silk ribbon is very thin and works beautifully with machine stitching, forming a loop for each petal on this project as you stitch over the tightly twisted ribbon. The flowers' petals are fragile-looking and no two turn out exactly the same. As you stitch over twists and folds of the ribbon, the flowers come to life.

SUPPLIES

bent-nose tweezers
7mm silk ribbon (1 yard green, ½ yard each of three flower colors)
ten 2mm beads for flower centers
clear monofilament thread
10″ of trim to edge the heart
1 yard of 7mm silk ribbon for scallop border
16 beads for scallop border
fabric, lace, and stuffing for the 5″ square pillow
5″ spring hoop
Optional: miniature opalescent sequins for enhancing background fabric

MACHINE SETUP

Stitch length: 0
Stitch width: 0
Feed dogs: down or covered
Presser foot: none
Top tension: a little looser than normal
Lower tension: normal
Needle: #70-10
Top thread: monofilament
Bobbin thread: regular bobbin thread

1. Using a washout pen, make a brief sketch of the flower and leaf placement on the background fabric. The finished ribbonwork will change slightly, so anticipate adding a few buds or leaves to balance the composition.

2. *Lazy daisy:* Start with the flower at the upper right. Each petal is formed by making a loop and tacking at the base and the tip of each petal like a handstitched lazy daisy. Begin by holding one end of the ribbon and making two twists. Stitch over the narrow twist to anchor the first petal near the flower center (Figure 6.6a). Leave room for a beaded center. Hold the

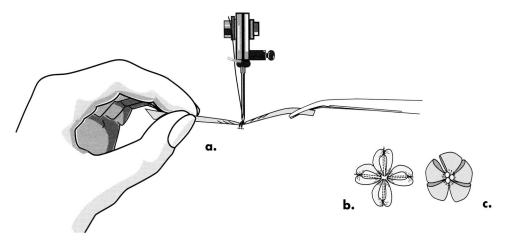

Figure 6.6 To attach silk ribbon to background fabric, stitch across a tight twist with short stitches (a). Create flowers by securing the ribbon at the base of each petal. For variety, some petals can be anchored at the tips of the petals like the traditional lazy daisy (b). Other petals are loops attached only at the center. A few beads in the center of some of the flowers provide a nice finishing touch (c).

ribbon aside while stitching out to the tip of the petal. Gently grip the ribbon with bent-nose tweezers to form a slight arch and stitch across the ribbon at the tip of the petal. Avoiding the ribbon, stitch back to the center of the flower and then over the twisted ribbon to make the other half of the petal (Figure 6.6b). Repeat until all the petals are done and then sew a few beads in the center individually to finish. The ribbon can be trimmed close to the tiny stitches that anchor it at the beginning and the end.

3. *Looped petals:* The next flower is a little larger and sits on the lower left. The petals are tacked only at the base, near the flower center. First stitch over the twisted ribbon at the base of the first petal. Make a ½″ loop in the ribbon and insert the closed tip of the tweezers inside the loop to hold it in tension while you stitch across a second twist to complete the petal at its base. Repeat to complete the flower and add beads in the center (Figure 6.6c).

4. *Buds:* The buds are made by stitching a length of knotted ribbon to the background. Tie a series of loose overhand knots in 7mm ribbon (Figure 6.7a). They should be close together but not tight (you may want to make minor adjustments before stitching). Stitch through the ribbon between each knot, placing the knots where you want to fill the background with buds (Figure 6.7b).

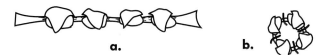

a.   b.

Figure 6.7 A cluster of buds can be represented by using a strand of silk ribbon that has overhand knots in it tied closely together. It is secured to the fabric by stitching through the ribbon in the space between the loosely tied knots.

5. *Beaded scallop border:* Stitch a 7mm silk ribbon to the background at ½″ intervals. Hold the ribbon flat with your left index finger while gripping the twisted section with bent-nose tweezers near the area to be stitched. Stitch a single bead over this twisted area, then stitch only on the background fabric for about ½″ to the spot for the next twist (Figure 6.8). Bead each twist before moving to the next one. Two loops can be added at each corner (made just like the petals in Step 3).

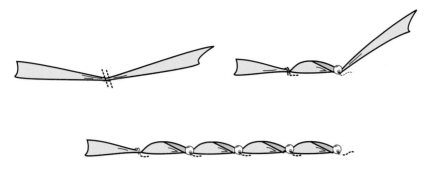

Figure 6.8 The border is made by simply stitching over the twisted intervals in the 7mm silk ribbon and stitching a single bead over each twist. Both steps are done before moving to the next interval. The fine ribbon twists to such a small size that it looks like the beads have been strung onto the ribbon.

6. *Leaves:* Study your floral arrangement and decide where you would like to add leaves. The places you decide on may be different than you originally planned, and that's OK. The natural placement is for each leaf to radiate from the center of each flower, but the leaves may come out at varying lengths. Stitch over the twisted ribbon to start (Figure 6.9a). Fold the ribbon under itself so it makes a point at the tip of the leaf and the ribbon comes out on the other half of the leaf. Stitch down the center of the leaf, on the background fabric, and continue over the ribbon and stop at the tip of the leaf (Figure 6.9b). Make the other half of the leaf by folding the ribbon opposite the first half. Stitch back to the base of the leaf and over the twisted base to finish (Figure 6.9c). You can make two or three leaves near each other with a continuous length of ribbon.

7. Stitch a decorative trim to outline the heart shape. You can add beads individually if they aren't already on the trim. The background can be embellished with miniature sequins of the same color. Stitch them as needed to fill in close to the leaves and flowers.

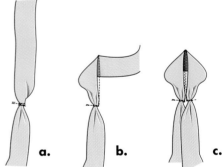

a.   **b.**   **c.**

Figure 6.9 Stitch over twisted ribbon (a); secure ribbon and stop at leaf tip (b); stitch back to base of leaf (c).

Button and Charm Necklace

My favorite crocheted button necklace makes a pleasant sound as the very old plastic buttons click and clack against each other. The shades of blue and grey look great with denim and are reminiscent of times when colors, like the economy, were grim. This project produces a necklace similar to my favorite blue-and-grey, with beads and buttons on the ends of the fringelike loops (Figure 6.10). It takes minimal skill with free-motion stitching. The necklace can be stitched to jump rings or else directly to the rings on a clasp.

To create your own button and charm treasure, search through your jewelry box, button jar, and bead box. You may find yourself sorting items for more than one necklace. Perhaps you have the right treasures to make one with all metallic pieces and another with all animals, flowers, or shades of a particular color. Isn't it great to finally use and enjoy the treasures you have saved for such a long time? I have used combinations of Czechoslovakian glass beads, metal beads, baby buttons, and charms to make the gold, silver, and black necklace shown in the photograph above and on page 56. It too makes a joyous sound.

Figure 6.10 The Button and Charm Necklace dangles an assortment of small items at the end of each loop.

SUPPLIES

#70-10 needle
5" or 7" spring hoop
two pieces of water-soluble stabilizer, 8" × 36" each
fine-tipped permanent pen (such as Pigma or Sharpie)
two pieces of white paper
polyester or metallic machine embroidery thread
YLI Candlelight metallic thread on a bobbin (or use #5 or #8 pearl cotton)
assortment of beads, buttons, charms that will slide up a #70-10 needle

MACHINE SETUP ....

Stitch length: 0

Stitch width: 0

Feed dogs: down or covered

Presser foot: none

Tension: the stitch is balanced, but the top is tightened slightly and the bobbin is loosened to accommodate the heavier thread

Needle size: #70-10

Top thread: metallic or polyester embroidery for strength

Bobbin thread: YLI Candlelight metallic thread

1. Determine the length of your necklace by draping a cord or cloth tape measure around your neck. Note that because of the nature of this technique, the necklace will finish 1″ to 2″ longer than the way it drapes. Draw a straight line the desired finished length on a piece of water-soluble stabilizer that is 8″ wide. Draw a line 1¼″ on each side of the first one (Figure 6.11). This is the guide for stitching fringe 1¼″ long.

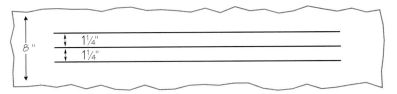

Figure 6.11 This is the pattern for the stitching lines that are drawn on water-soluble stabilizer for the Button and Charm Necklace.

....

2. Fuse a second piece of water-soluble stabilizer to the first. Using glue stick, glue a 4mm jump ring or clasp to each end of the line you drew first (the middle line). If using a jump ring, keep the split facing away from the necklace so it will be easier to attach a closure later.

3. Place the stabilizer in a 5″ or 7″ spring hoop at one end of the necklace; you will move it as the work progresses along the length of the necklace. When it is time to move the hoop, lower the needle into the stabilizer. Reposition the hoop and carefully spring it into place, keeping the stabilizer smooth. Most of the time you can avoid the beads already attached, but when necessary, you can hoop over most seed beads without causing damage to them or the stitching. When you need to avoid hooping over a large or fragile bead, place the inner ring of the hoop so the opening between the handles is on either side of the bead.

4. The main stitching line will be referred to as the chain. Take the first stitch inside the jump ring or clasp and pull up the bobbin thread. Stitch over the ring and back into it a second time, making sure to stitch over the thread tails (Figure 6.12). The first 4″ on each end of the chain will have only small beads. Stitch along the drawn

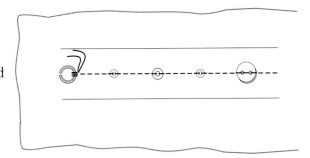

Figure 6.12 Take stitches to secure the threads to the jump ring and then proceed to attach beads and buttons as you create the first 4″ of the necklace.

....

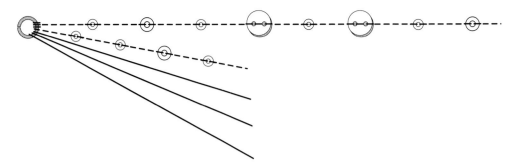

Figure 6.21 When you reach the opposite end, anchor the stitching to the other jump ring and then stitch the next strand going back to the other end.

5. When you reach the opposite end, stitch into and out of the jump ring or clasp twice. Turn the work around so you can begin the next strand (Figure 6.21). Continue sewing the rest of the strands.

6. To finish, stitch into and out of the jump ring or clasp a few times and remove the work from the machine, leaving 6″ thread tails. Secure the thread tails with two surgeon's knots (see Page 17) and seam sealant.

7. Trim the water-soluble stabilizer to within ¼″ of the stitching. Soak and rinse the necklace in warm water until all the stabilizer is removed. Move it gently so the strands don't tangle.

STITCHING TIPS AND IDEAS

• Use Madeira's Neon polyester machine embroidery thread on the top and in the bobbin to make a strong yet delicate-looking necklace.

• Use construction thread on the top and in the bobbin (for smaller seed beads use construction thread on the bobbin and use a fine thread through the needle).

• Wind double threads on the bobbin to add interest and bulk to the necklace. Sometimes sewing with two threads in the bobbin is easier than running two threads through a single needle while beading.

Bedazzled Note Cards

Note cards and gift tags have a professional touch when made using whimsical hole punches and scissors that create special patterns. The festive ornament pictured features a technique that involves "stitching in the air."

With a combination of free-motion machine stitchery, a few beads, and novelty hole punches and scissors, you can create quick one-of-a-kind note cards and gift tags. Use a heavyweight paper known as cover stock or cardstock. If you want to work with premade cards with a variety of cutouts, see the Resources list at the back of the book.

A variety of hole-punch patterns by Uchida come in two sizes, finishing approximately ½″ and ¾″ square (Figure 6.22). Using these patterns is less time-consuming than cutting out your own pattern by hand. Edges can be trimmed with Fiskars Paper Edgers (or similar scissors) to expose a colored strip of paper or ribbon glued to the back half of the card. Twelve different edgers offer lots of design possibilities and will give your project a professional finish (Figure 6.23). They can make the difference between handmade and homemade.

Figure 6.22 Marvy/Uchida Jumbo Craft Punches can be used to cut out appealing shapes from paper.

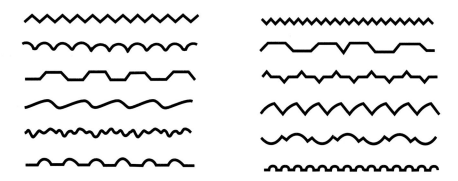

Figure 6.23 These are 12 patterns cut by Fiskars Paper Edgers, which offer many possibilities when making your own cards, bookmarks, and gift tags.

SUPPLIES

cardstock or premade blank cards
embroidery thread
seed beads
hole punches
paper scissors for fancy cuts
fabric scraps
glue stick

MACHINE SETUP

Stitch length: 0
Stitch width: 0
Feed dogs: down or covered
Presser foot: darning
Upper tension: normal
Lower tension: normal
Needle size: #70-10
Top thread: rayon or metallic
Bobbin thread: regular cotton bobbin thread

1. Cut the cardstock to the desired size. This may be determined by the size of envelopes you have. Cut 7″ × 6¼″ for letter-size envelopes and 8″ × 9¼″ for legal-size envelopes.

2. Wash your hands and then fold each card, matching the corners and making a crease with your fingers (since body oils and lotions may stain the paper, wash your hands first). Make a sharper crease by going over it with a burnishing tool or the rounded handle on a pair of scissors.

3. Use a hole punch to cut a design in the paper or cut your own with a utility knife.

4. Dab glue stick around the edges of the design, on the back side. Place a scrap of fabric underneath to cover the cutout area(s). Now glue a piece of plain paper to the back side of the fabric to stabilize it while stitching.

5. With minimal stitching, attach beads individually within or around the design (Figure 6.24). You can combine free-motion stitching with beading so you will only have to tie off the stitching a few times. To write a message, first draw lines and write the words with an air pen (Figure 6.25). By the time you finish stitching, the lines will have disappeared. Alternatively, use Clotilde's air-erasable pen to remove the ink without damage to the paper. Like the disappearing pens made by the same company, this type of pen has a nylon tip for superfine lines. Use a darning foot to help steady your work and move the card as if the needle were a writing tool.

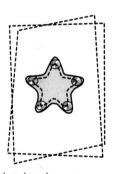

Figure 6.24 Simple beading and stitching by sewing machine can be added to cutouts backed with fabric. Paper punches by Marvy/Uchida were used for these designs.

6. To finish the card, use glue stick to glue another piece of cardstock behind the beadwork. Use 3½″ × 6¼″ for letter size and 4″ × 9″ for legal size. Smaller cards may be cut longer so the extra length can fold over the back of the stitching instead of your cutting a separate backing. Stitch the layers together with a small zigzag or a simple decorative stitch around all four sides. Trim the edges with the paper edgers.

Figure 6.25 Finish a greeting card by covering the stitching on the back side with another piece of cardstock. Sew the two layers together using a zigzag stitch for a clean and simple finish.

Beaded Ornament

This ornament features the very things that avid beaders loathe: plastic craft beads. These lowly beads are the most appropriate type for festive ornaments because of their size, colors, and sparkle. I think they are attractive in all their plastic splendor when combined with metallic threads. The gold or silver rings on which the ornaments are based are thin 3″ metal bracelets found in children's stores or inexpensive jewelry boutiques. You may occasionally find 2″ and 1″ sizes, as well as the 3″ size in a variety of colors.

A favorite bead to use is the paddle bead, which has six paddle shapes radiating from the center. Tri-beads have three rounded shapes extending beyond the hole. In most cases, the smaller size of each type of plastic bead is the right size. Remember, you are limited to using beads less than ¼″ thick. Any size sequin with a hole can be used. I like to use metallic thread in the bobbin and a similar color of rayon in the needle. This is a good time to experiment with different thread combinations. Note that the ridges on the bracelets hold the stitches in place. You will appreciate how the sewing machine's thread tension holds everything taught, producing great results as you "stitch in air."

Figure 6.26 Plastic craft beads combine with metallic threads to produce a sparkling ornament.

SUPPLIES

3″ gold ring (bracelet) for each ornament
assorted plastic beads and sequins
metallic and rayon embroidery threads
#70-10 needles
gold thread for hanging loops

MACHINE SETUP

Stitch length: 0
Stitch width: 0
Feed dogs: down or covered
Presser foot: none
Upper tension: normal (balanced stitch desired)
Lower tension: normal
Needle size: #70-10
Top thread: rayon
Bobbin thread: metallic

1. Lower the presser bar to engage the top tension.

2. Use gold rayon in the needle and a gold metallic thread in the bobbin. Tie and anchor the threads to the ring.

3. Raise the presser bar and move the ring so the needle is in the center. Lower the presser bar and sew into and out of a ¼″ clear paddle bead. Raise the presser bar and move the ring to the opposite side. Lower the presser bar and stitch to anchor the threads on the ring.

4. Repeat the above technique, working your way around the ring as if adding spokes to a wheel one pair after another on opposite sides (Figure 6.27). You will be surprised how fast this one goes. This is an unusual ornament with numerous spokes of thread, each a single stitch (Bernina owners will cherish the knee-lift when stitching this ornament). Tie on a hanging loop made from gold thread.

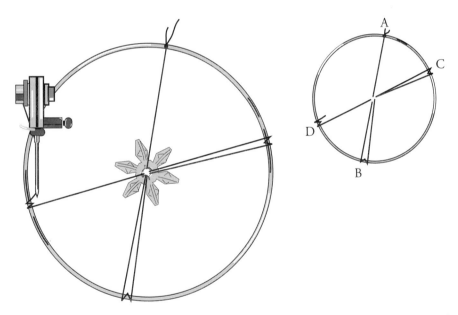

Figure 6.27 A single stitch produces each "spoke," working in opposite directions from a center paddle bead.

Chapter 7
·····•·····

EDGES & FRINGES

It is possible to stitch beaded fringes on the sewing machine, and you will find the methods outlined in this chapter quite innovative. You will learn how to make a beaded edge quickly with a machine foot, attach charms individually, create a beaded heirloom edge, and machine-stitch beaded fringe.

◀ You can add dazzling beaded edging or fringe to the simplest of sewing projects. From top left, an envelope purse with couched prestrung beads, an heirloom-edged bag, a "charming" zippered case, and a scarf are enhanced by beads.

Prestrung Beaded Edge

A quick method for applying a beaded edging uses prestrung beads and a machine foot with a deep groove on the underside. Look in your accessory box for a foot used for sewing over piping or cording. You might find that an invisible zipper foot attachment works for a smaller size bead. The beads must slide smoothly under the foot, and you may need to change the needle position to go over the beads. Creative Feet's Pearls 'N Piping foot sews on ⅛" and ¼" pearls, cross-locked beads, piping, prestrung rhinestones, and cords. It comes with adapters for low shank, high shank, Singer slant, and Kenmore tall. Bernina sewing machines also require a Bernina low shank adapter. The setup that follows allows you to sew the string of beads on top of the fabric in gently curving lines as well as on the edge of the fabric.

SUPPLIES

prestrung beads (2mm to 4mm—or larger if the stitch width is wide enough)
decorative thread or one that matches fabric
#70-10 machine needle

MACHINE SETUP

Stitch length: the length of the beads
Stitch width: a little wider than the beads
Feed dogs: up
Presser foot: for cording, piping, or beading
Upper tension: a little looser than normal
Lower tension: normal
Needle size: #70-10
Top thread: rayon, metallic, or monofilament
Bobbin thread: to match fabric

1. Attach the foot for the beading and make sure the beads slide under it smoothly. Remove the thread from the top and the bobbin case. Manually turn the handwheel, checking to see that the needle clears the beads with the zigzag stitch. Thread the machine and sew a sample to test your setup. Write the settings on the swatch and save it for reference with your machine's manual.

2. Place the fabric under the foot with the finished edge slightly under the inside of the left toe in the beading foot (Figure 7.1). Slide the string of beads under the foot. The beginning and ending stitches can be tied off by taking tiny straight stitches

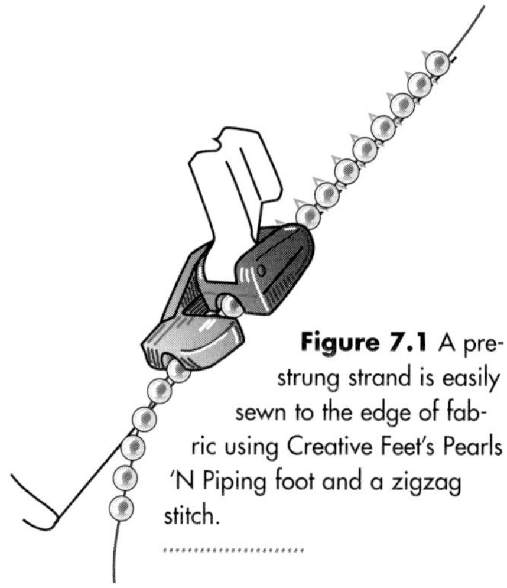

Figure 7.1 A prestrung strand is easily sewn to the edge of fabric using Creative Feet's Pearls 'N Piping foot and a zigzag stitch.

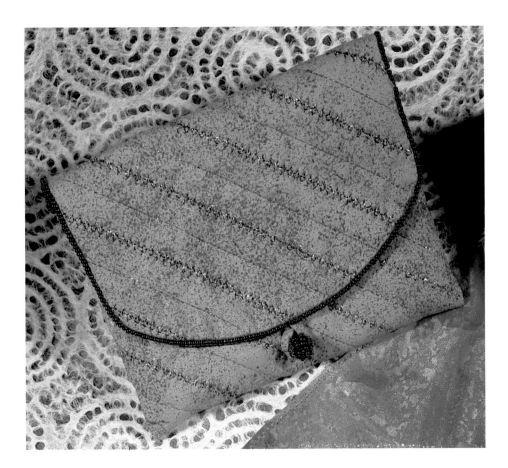

with an extreme left needle position, or they can be tied later by hand using a granny knot with hemostats (see page 18).

3. Sew over the bead strand with a zigzag stitch, barely catching the edge of the fabric on the left side of the beads. For a slightly different look, sew the beads so they are completely on the fabric, even with the edge.

4. If necessary, you can break the beads in the seam areas with pliers so only the connecting threads will be secured in the seams (see Chapter 5 for instruction on breaking beads).

Chapter 8

• • • • • • • • • • •

BEAD EMBROIDERY

You can enrich the appearance of printed fabric with flourishes of beading and embroidery. Together they bring attention to necklines, yokes, cuffs, and collars. On a simple garment like a vest, the entire print may be enhanced and a special beaded cinch strap can be added on the back. Like embroidery, beading on a printed fabric gives you the opportunity to change the color scheme or to repeat certain colors so that the finished piece is exactly right for you. This is your chance to alter gorgeous prints that come in colors that won't quite work for you or to add a zing of your favorite hue to a print that needs to be livened up.

TIPS FOR BEAD EMBROIDERY BY MACHINE

• Consider using designer upholstery fabrics, lace, and hand-painted fabrics. A piece of fabric that starts out formal and classic may be made glitzy and festive by the style and amount of beadwork applied. Many fabrics feature rich patterns for embellishment, and often the amount of beading and embroidery you do on a piece is determined by how much time you have and your willpower to stop. Note that a carefully planned conservative amount can be very effective. A heavily worked piece can be a show-stopper and is better suited for evening wear and fashion shows.

• Select the fabric and use a washout marker to draw the outline and seam lines for each pattern piece selected for embellishment. Cut the pieces out *after* the stitchery is finished since you will need extra fabric for hooping. Decide on the appropriate stabilizer and hoop for the fabric using the information given in Chapter 4 (Table 4.1). Additional beadwork may be added over seam lines later.

• Keep the embellishment away from the seams so that the foot will ride smoothly when you assemble the garment, or use a zipper foot for sewing where the beading is close to the seam. If you want to include machine embroidery with rayon, cotton, or metallic threads, do this before doing the beading since it will be easier to move the hoop before the beads are on. The beads may be attached by couching over a strand of prestrung beads, or they may be stitched on individually. Consider using buttons and charms. Tie off all the thread tails and assemble the garment as usual.

• Machine beading on single knits and sweater knits is easily done, but it is crucial to use the right stabilizer (see Chapter 4, Table 4.1). Using Do Sew or Trace-A-Pattern on the back of the knit and hooping both layers with a spring hoop will allow you to do any kind of beading and embroidery without distorting the knit.

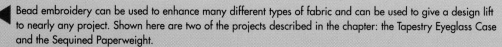

◀ Bead embroidery can be used to enhance many different types of fabric and can be used to give a design lift to nearly any project. Shown here are two of the projects described in the chapter: the Tapestry Eyeglass Case and the Sequined Paperweight.

Ultrasuede Paisley Appliqués

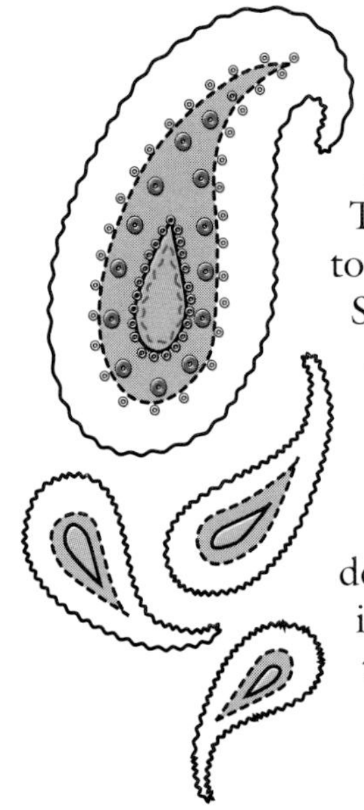

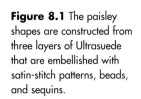

These classic appliqué shapes are constructed from three graduated layers of Ultrasuede (Figure 8.1). The rich color and texture of the fabric distinguishes these appliqués from those made from "lesser" fabrics. The beadwork is combined with automatic decorative machine stitching to give the illusion of fine details that the paisley print is known for. Sequins, seed beads, and bugle beads adorn the fabric shapes. The back side of each shape is later coated with Press 'N Wear bonding film, allowing the appliqués to be placed on various garments or projects and then safely stored when not in use.

The idea of making removable appliqués is especially useful for various decorative holiday pieces that may be applied to your favorite garments. It is much easier to reapply the adhesive to the appliqué than it is to replace the embellished garment. The nonraveling quality of Ultrasuede is an added bonus in this project.

Figure 8.1 The paisley shapes are constructed from three layers of Ultrasuede that are embellished with satin-stitch patterns, beads, and sequins.

SUPPLIES

3½" × 10" of Ultrasuede fabric in four colors
four colors of seed beads (approximately 160 total)
twelve ¼" bugle beads
three colors of sequins (100 total)
monofilament thread
regular machine embroidery bobbin thread
four colors of rayon or metallic machine embroidery thread matching the fabric
selection of satin-stitch patterns for the sewing machine
5" or 7" spring hoop
tear-away stabilizer
water-soluble stabilizer
paper-backed fusible web
Press 'N Wear bonding film
pinking, wavy, or scallop-edged fabric scissors or rotary blade

MACHINE SETUP

Stitch length: satin stitch (about 2.5)
Stitch width: 3–5
Feed dogs: up
Presser foot: appliqué open-toe
Upper tension: slightly loose
Lower tension: normal
Needle: #70-10
Top thread: rayon or metallic
Bobbin thread: regular bobbin thread or match fabric

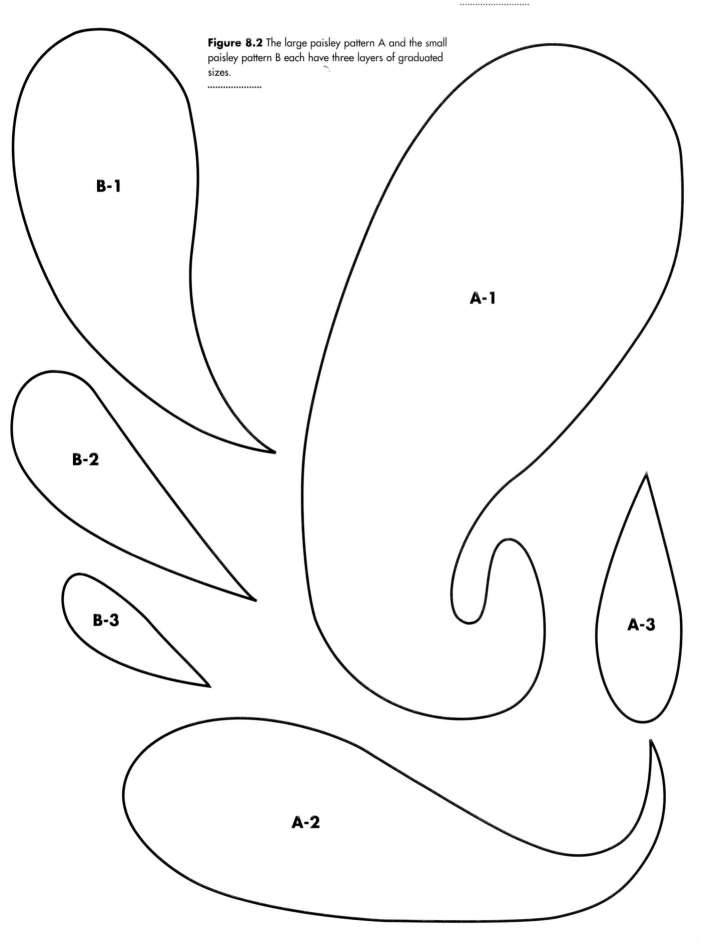

Figure 8.2 The large paisley pattern A and the small paisley pattern B each have three layers of graduated sizes.

1. Using the pattern in Figure 8.2, make cardboard templates for the three large and three small paisley shapes in graduated sizes. Put freezer paper or Totally Stable stabilizer on top of the book page and trace the paisley shapes. Iron the paper or stabilizer onto cardboard and cut out your patterns. Since each paisley motif has three layers, decide which color of Ultrasuede you will use for each layer. Plan a different combination for each one.

2. Flip the large and small paisley templates over and trace around them on the wrong side of the Ultrasuede fabric using washout pen or pencil. (The templates are flipped over because you are working on the *wrong* side of the fabric.)

3. Trace around the templates (backward) of the two smaller patterns on the paper backing of fusible web. Press the fusible web on the back of the four colors of Ultrasuede following the manufacturer's instructions. Each shape can be cut out with a different style of scissors or rotary blade (pinking, wavy, scallop). Stack the three colors for each paisley. This is the last time to make changes in the color of each layer. For each paisley, fuse two layers together, then fuse the assembly to the third layer.

4. Place one paisley on a piece of tear-away stabilizer. This will keep the fabric from puckering during the satin stitching. Choose an embroidery thread and satin-stitch pattern (Figure 8.3). Use it on all the paisleys at a different place on each one. Start sewing near the point of the shape so you won't have to match the stitching at the end. Change the stitch pattern as you like. Select a second thread color and another satin-stitch pattern and use them on contrasting layers. These satin-stitch patterns start looking like beads because of their size.

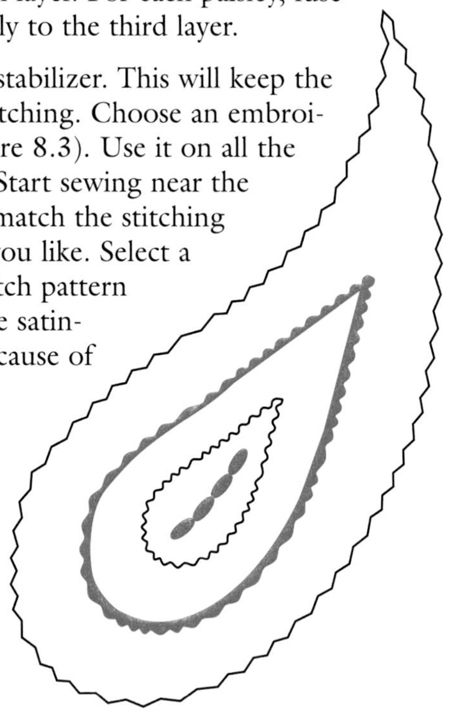

Figure 8.3 This assembly of the small paisley pattern B shows two different stitch patterns represented in thick colored lines.

5. Remove all of the tear-away stabilizer and pin the paisley assemblies to water-soluble stabilizer. Center the paisley when you put the stabilizer into a hoop.

6. Before doing the remaining instructions, change the machine setup as follows:

MACHINE SETUP ....

    Stitch length: 0
    Stitch width: 0
    Feed dogs: down or covered
    Presser foot: none
    Upper tension: slightly loose
    Lower tension: normal
    Needle: #60-8
    Top thread: monofilament
    Bobbin thread: regular bobbin thread or thread to match fabric

7. Choose from your selection of beads and sequins and attach them individually at intervals suggested by the stitch pattern. The paisleys shown in the photograph below use smoke-colored monofilament thread because of the medium-to-dark fabric. For light fabric use clear monofilament. Whenever possible, stitch inconspicuously next to previous stitching or the fabric edge. You can alternate the color of beads or sequins for added interest as done on the large paisley shown.

8. Bugle beads can be attached individually in the following way (Figure 8.4): Take four or five small stitches to secure the thread to the fabric. Slide a

The rich color and texture of the Ultrasuede fabric beautifully sets off the intricate beadwork and stitching.

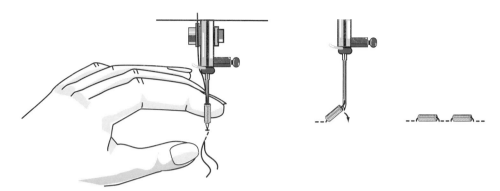

Figure 8.4 Stitching bugle beads individually is just like attaching round beads except that after taking one stitch into the bead, the next stitch must be equal to the length of the bugle bead away from the previous stitch. This allows the bead to lie flat.

bugle bead up the machine needle and plant the needle in the fabric. Turn the handwheel until the needle is up again. Move the hoop slightly so the next stitch will put the needle about ¼″ away from the last stitch (the approximate length of the bugle bead). The placement of this second stitch also dictates which direction the bugle bead will lay. If the stitch is too long, the thread will show and the bead will slide on it. If the stitch is too short, the bead will not lay down and the thread will break from wear.

Like seed beads, bugle beads can be attached on a strand. This would be the method of choice when you want to fill an area with a precise pattern, whether the beads are to be oriented end to end or side by side. Simply stitch over the strand after each bead is in place. To secure the beginning of the strand, stitch through it with tiny machine stitches. Once the strand feels secure, cover the stitching with bead-work. Secure the end of the strand by holding it near the beads or another inconspicuous spot and stitching over it. Another way to secure the beginning and ending strands is to take them to the back side by threading through a hand needle and tying off by hand.

9. Cut the paisley shapes away from the water-soluble stabilizer, leaving a ¼″ border. Dampen the back side with a wet towel to remove the rest. If the stabilizer gets too wet and turns to gel, soak the paisley in water until the stabilizer is completely removed and then air-dry.

10. The paisley shapes may be stitched to a garment or else a bonding film may be applied on the back so they are repositionable. (Follow the manu-facturer's directions for the bonding film to prevent undesirable results. For example, Press 'N Wear's maker suggests *not* to apply appliqués backed with their product to leather and fine fabrics—silk, chiffon, satin, etc.—because it will mar the finish. Note that if an appliqué with bonding film is applied to a garment of 100% polyester or is left on a garment of other fabric content overnight, it may become permanently attached.) The appliqués should be stored on the original backing paper and in a plastic bag to keep the adhesive fresh from one holiday to the next. A second layer of bonding film can be applied easily when the stickiness of the original layer is no longer adequate. With removable appliqués, you will find countless ways to enjoy your machine-beaded work.

Tapestry Eyeglass Case

This project is rich with Renaissance colors from the tapestry fabric used and is enhanced by the glass beads that were all attached by machine stitching. The beads intensify and sometimes change the original colors of the fabric. You will find that as you study fabric prints, you will envision many ways to embellish them by machine. This eyeglass case project is small in size, but the time invested can become monumental if you get carried away with the bead embroidery. All of the beading on this project is done by couching over a strand of custom-strung beads or by attaching the beads individually. These two methods are thoroughly covered in Chapters 5 and 6.

I found some bonuses associated with working on the pricey tapestry fabric. First, it is sturdy and doesn't require interlining. Second, the countless machine stitches are truly invisible and the black thread used for stringing the beads is camouflaged when you run it parallel to the dark warp threads of the tapestry fabric. This is a convenience when moving from one section to another because you can just couch down the Nymo stringing thread rather than having to cut it. The monofilament stitching seems to bury the Nymo in the weave of the fabric.

SUPPLIES

smoke monofilament (grey)
rayon or cotton bobbin thread in black (or some other dark color)
Nymo # B
#10 beading needle
beeswax
tapestry fabric
lining (velveteen or other plush woven fabric)
construction thread
10" wooden hoop
assortment of seed beads, bugle beads, and flat beads

Sequined Paperweight

This paperweight is a novel way to display and enjoy bead embroidery. The one shown at left uses wrinkled silk fabric, which became more interesting after I dyed it. There were a few places where the dyed color wasn't exactly what I wanted, but these spots disappeared under a shower of antique sequins and machine stitching.

You can usually find an assortment of glass and acrylic paperweights at cross-stitch or hand stitchery shops. See the Resources section for additional information. The paperweights have almost ⅛" under the dome so you can use embroidery and seed beads; if necessary, pad the fabric with a thin fleece before assembling. I hand-dyed a piece of finely wrinkled silk for this project, but you can use any lightweight fabric.

SUPPLIES

background fabric
5" spring hoop
fusible tricot
sequins
monofilament
bobbin thread
paperweight
10" × 10" piece of silk, dyed or plain

MACHINE SETUP

Stitch length: 0
Stitch width: 0
Feed dogs: down or covered
Presser foot: none
Upper tension: slightly loose
Lower tension: normal
Needle size: # 70-10
Top thread: smoke monofilament
Bobbin thread: regular bobbin thread

1. Stabilize the background fabric by pressing fusible tricot on the back.

2. To help choose the best section of the fabric for embellishing, use a manila file folder to make a cutout that is the same size as the outline of the paperweight. (Generally, you will stop beading ¼″ from this outline.) Move the template around the fabric until you find a section that appeals to you. Make sure to allow another ½″ around for finishing. Draw the outline on the fabric with a washout pen.

3. Place the fabric in a 5″ spring hoop. Using one of the stitching methods given in Chapter 6, stitch sequins on the fabric. You can attach them separately, in stacked layers of contrasting colors, or attach them in overlapping piles. The silk I used has miniature rows of wrinkles, so I hid all the stitching in the valleys of the wrinkles. Additional satin stitching can be added in varying widths.

4. Cut out the beaded fabric so you will have about ½″ extra on all sides. Zigzag stitch on the edge to strengthen. Run a gathering stitch by hand close to the edge. If you have room, put a layer of fleece between the fabric and the cardboard so it will fit snug to the glass. Pull the gathers tight and take a few stitches to draw in the sides tighter. Place the embroidery in the paperweight and apply the adhesive-backed cork to cover the back of the stitchery.

Chapter 9
. . . .
SERGER BEADING PROJECTS

You probably know that a microwave isn't just for warming up leftovers, but did you know that a serger isn't just for making neat seams? The projects in this chapter use the tight serger chain of a rolled-edge setup, combining novelty threads and beads. The instructions that follow indicate using a standard serger presser foot. I find that removing the foot makes the serging much easier, but if you choose to do this you must exercise caution since the needle is not surrounded by a presser foot. This approach is preferred by many, but it is not for the faint of heart. Note that the presser bar must still be lowered to engage the correct tensions, the cutting blade is raised, and the rest of the machine setup is the same.

◀ If you have a serger, try making serger necklaces and the serger chain brooch and earrings by following the instructions in this chapter. A variety of beads and threads can be used for these projects.

Serger Chain Necklace

Making serger necklaces (Figure 9.1) is all the rage since Judi Maddigan, of San Jose, California, originated the idea of making serged and beaded cords by incorporating beads into a cord while serging a rolled hem over fish line. Her work is featured in Jackie Dodson's *How to Make Soft Jewelry.*

Figure 9.1 This five-strand serger necklace is made using one long piece of beaded serger chain.

SUPPLIES

seed beads, semiprecious nuggets, shells
rayon, polyester, or metallic thread (use the difficult or heavier threads in the loopers)
6-lb-test fishing line
Big Eye Needle
findings: two 3″ eye pins, two bell caps, one necklace clasp
round-nose pliers

MACHINE SETUP

Stitch length: 1
Stitch width: for narrow rolled edge
Differential: normal
Presser foot: standard one or none at all
Lower knife: if you can, move it to the left for a rolled edge
Upper knife: move up, out of the way
Right needle tension: normal
Upper looper tension: normal to start
Lower looper tension: tight, as you would set for a rolled edge
Needle size: # 70-10 (size for regular serging of garments)
Right needle thread: rayon or polyester
Top looper thread: any machine embroidery thread or heavier metallic thread (like Candlelight)
Lower looper thread: any machine embroidery thread

1. String the fishing line with a random assortment of beads. A Big Eye Needle will make the stringing easy. Estimate that you will use about 30 beads for a 25″ length (and you may want 15 to 20 lengths total). *Do not cut the fishing line* because you will be serging on it, reeling off more as it is needed.

2. Thread your serger with rayon or metallic threads. Heavier weights of threads like YLI's Candlelight will give you more dramatic results, making

heavier serger cords. Try using a heavy metallic in one of the loopers. Use a Thread Palette on the top looper stand so you can run threads from multiple spools through each looper (see the Resources list). Adjust the serger for a rolled edge, using the right needle. Using three different colors of threads will facilitate tension adjustments.

3. If possible, raise the cutting blade. Raise the presser foot and insert the filler cord (fishing line) so that you can serge over it for at least 4″ to make sure the tensions are set correctly. You can make a tighter thread chain by tightening the upper looper tension slightly and holding the chain firmly as you serge. *Now* is the time to fine-tune the machine setup, not halfway through the necklace.

4. Slide one bead up the filler cord (fishing line) and swing it to the left of the foot, making a loop with the filler cord (Figure 9.2). Lower the foot and serge over the filler cord until the loop clears the back of the foot, about 1″.

5. Raise the foot. Eliminate the loop by pulling on the filler cord (fishing line) in *front* of the serger presser foot. Now the bead is snug against the serger chain. Continue serging and adding beads until you reach the total length needed for the necklace. Each necklace is made up of 20 lengths (approximately 14 yards total for a 25″ long necklace). Consider rethreading the loopers so you can serge half of the strand (7 yards) in a slightly different color scheme.

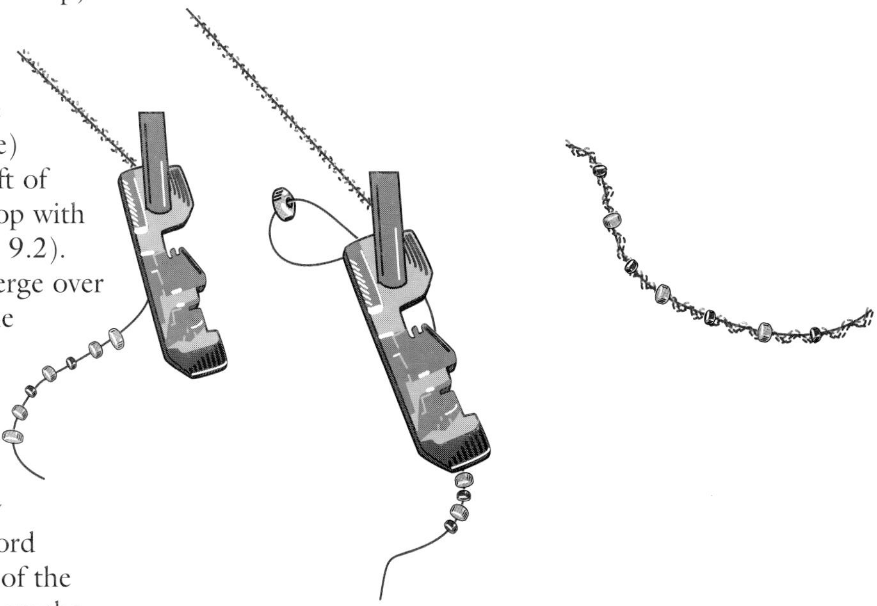

Figure 9.2 To make a beaded serger chain, string seed beads onto fishing line then serge over the fishing line and pull up one or more beads on a loop of fishing line. Continue serging equal to the length of beads pulled up, then serge on the fishing line. Pull slightly to snug the beads to the serger chain.

6. At this point you can experiment with pulling up several beads at a time to form a loop (Figure 9.3). For beads larger than 3mm you will have to serge a distance equal to the length of the bead without catching the filler cord. Then serge over the filler cord (fishing line) and repeat. Pebbles or nuggets of semiprecious stones are great in addition to glass beads. When using beads that are all smaller than 2mm, you can serge slowly without stopping to slide the beads. With practice, you will be able to feed the beads by pulling the filler cord and allowing one or more beads to slide down toward the needle while it is in the up position.

Figure 9.3 This serger chain shows single beads and bead groupings that form loops along the serged thread chain.

7. To finish the necklace, fold the full length of the beaded serger chain in half, in half again, in half again, and so on until the multiple strands reach the desired finished length. Bend a wire or eye pin around the loops of serger chain at each end of the necklace and pull it through a bell cap (Figure 9.4). When the strands are pulled tightly into the cap, bend and cut the wire. Form a loop using round-nose pliers. Attach a clasp and enjoy wearing your serger creation!

Figure 9.4 Finish the serger necklace by pulling the serger cord snug into a bell cap with eye pin bent into a loop at one end. Bend another loop in the eye pin at the top of the bell cap and then attach the loop to a clasp.

Serger Chain Brooch and Earrings

This earring and brooch ensemble (courtesy of Marjorie Howe, San Diego, California) is a blending of twisted fibers and beaded serger chain. This will take us one step beyond the serger chain.

1. First hoop a double layer of tulle with a piece of water-soluble stabilizer on top. Decide what shape you want for the brooch or earrings—round, triangular, free-form, whatever—and draw that shape on the stabilizer. This technique could also be used directly on a garment or other background fabric.

2. Take a strand of the beaded serger cord (about 2 yards) and fold it in half twice. Twist the cord until it starts to kink and coil back on itself. Now it is of a substantial thickness to work with.

3. Take a single stitch in the hooped layers and pull up the bobbin thread. Take four tiny stitches, locking the threads. Stitch one end of the twisted cord to one of the design areas on the stabilizer. Couch the twisted cord in the design area, filling in the shape. Twist the cord more as needed and anchor with stitching.

4. Finish by stitching the ends of the twisted cords down with several small stitches, burying the cord within the dimensional work. Cut the finished shape with a ¼" border on the fabric and then fold the excess under when attaching it to a jewelry finding or when attaching a piece of Ultrasuede for a clean finish with E-6000 adhesive.

Beaded Fringe

This unique fringe is a great way to use your serger to manufacture a corded fringe in custom colors with your choice of beads and dangles. For this project (unlike the previous serger projects) you don't need a filler cord unless you want it for added strength or color. Also, for this project keep the presser foot on.

SUPPLIES

larger seed beads, semiprecious nuggets, shells
rayon, polyester, or metallic thread (use difficult or heavier threads in the loopers)
Big Eye Needle or other threader

MACHINE SETUP

Stitch length: 1
Stitch width: for narrow rolled edge
Differential: normal
Presser foot: standard
Lower knife: if you can, move it to the left for a rolled edge
Upper knife: move up, out of the way
Right needle tension: normal
Upper looper tension: normal to start
Lower looper tension: tight, as you would set for a rolled edge
Needle size: # 70-10 (size for regular serging of garments)
Right needle thread: rayon or polyester
Top looper thread: any machine embroidery thread or heavier metallic (like
    Candlelight)
Lower looper thread: any machine embroidery thread

1. Thread the serger with three different threads in the needle and loopers. Set the tensions as suggested and then tighten the top tension a little more to make a tighter serger chain. Serge off a few inches and check the tensions. Serge several yards of chain. You can always make more if you need it.

2. Determine the finished width of the fringe and add ¼" for seam allowance. Make a loom from a wire clothes hanger. Bend it into a U-shape to the desired width. Cut a ½" strip of cardboard and poke two holes the same width as the U-shape. Slide this onto the loom to keep the wires from flexing to a different width.

3. Loop one end of the serger chain into a Big Eye Needle or other needle threader. String an assortment of buttons, beads, and/or charms onto the serger chain.

4. Tie the cord near the "open" end of the loom. Wrap the loom with the serger cord. Pull up a bead at regular intervals while you are wrapping so they will always hang on the same side of the loom.

5. Machine-stitch on the inside of the loom on the side opposite from the beads, leaving about ¼″ for insertion into a seam. This can be done without a presser foot, or you can use a zipper foot if you need a little help guiding the fringe. Remove the cardboard and slide off the fringe. With practice, you can wrap and sew, sliding the finished fringe off the back of the loom as you run out of room. The finished fringe can then be topstitched on a project, with decorative stitching or with a ribbon on top to hide the first securing stitches. It can also be glued to a basket or covered box.

TIP: If you like to use a serger for beading, the Universal Pearl Sewing Foot makes it easy to serge beading or sequins to the edge of fabrics. It will make quick work of edging bridal veils. Put monofilament thread in the top looper and thread to match the fabric in the needle and lower looper. The serger sews effortlessly over fabrics like netting, lace, and knits.

ARTISTS' GALLERY

Right: The lingerie case by Marcia Pollard of Glendora, California, blends machine embroidery and bead embroidery in a classic design. **Lower left:** The top brooch, by the author, is encrusted with glass and metal beads and lapis lazuli over ripples of embroidery with metallic threads. Mary Shaudies of Corpus Christi, Texas, created two brooches of geometric shapes. The "fabric" of the work is machine stitched then machine beaded. **Lower right:** Bambi Stalder of Penngrove, California, embroidered and beaded her marbleized fabric for the cover of this opulent box.

Left: Couched strands of beads and machine stitching embellish this book by Bambi Stalder, of Penngrove, California. The cover is handmade paper with painted textures. Gina Butler from Oklahoma City, Oklahoma, has woven then machine stitched the watchband for the antique watch face. Antique steel cut beads are also stitched on the band. **Lower right:** This lower, front view of a "collar" by the author is edged with loops of yarn and machine embroidery threads. They dangle beads, charms, and dozens of miniature bells that produce a pleasant ringing when worn.

APPENDIX

Most of the information in this section pertains to hand beading supplies and methods. Such information my be helpful if your work pushes the limits of basic threads and techniques used in beading by machine. By learning more about these supplies you might be inspired to try new twists on the basic projects presented in this book.

NECKLACE AND BRACELET LENGTHS

Choker	14″
Princess	16″–18″
Matinee	20″–24″
Opera	30″–34″
Rope	40″–45″
Lariat or sautoir	48″ or longer (tied in a knot)
Bracelet	7″
Ankle bracelet	9″
Boot bracelet	13″–14″

MORE HANDY TOOLS

Chapter 4 introduces the basic tools that are specific for machine beading. Other traditional and innovative tools used in beadwork by hand and machine are described here. Once you have done some of the beading projects in this book, you will have a feel for which "extra" tools will make your beading efforts easier and more rewarding.

- *Beading boards* are invaluable for stringing. They are plastic and are flocked (in neutral grey) to create a surface that keeps beads from rolling. The U-shaped groove is marked in ¹⁄₂″ and 1″ increments in both directions, with 0 being the center front of the necklace. These markings make it easy to design the layout of the beads before stringing. These boards come in different sizes, with compartments for holding extra beads. Multistrand boards have five U-shaped slots for planning up to five strands at the same time (see photo on page 24).

- A *bead design template* is a transparent plastic template that lets you create your design on paper even if you don't have all the beads on hand. The template measures 10³⁄₈″ × 6¹⁄₄″. The curved end with markings at ¹⁄₁₆″ and ¹⁄₁₀″ increments helps you to draw the strand and lay out the pattern. Cutouts for common bead shapes and sizes and an assortment of clasps and bead tips help you draw every detail with ease (see photo on page 24).

- *Bead Nabber* by LoRan is a fingertip tool that holds seed beads for easy skewering and eliminates trolling for beads in the container. The tool protects your finger from the needle's point while its textured, tacky tip holds the beads for stringing.

- *Quilter's thimbles* are made from a variety of materials. The soft leather styles help grip the needle for pulling it through the fabric, while the plastic ones have concave tips or an indentation near the end where the needle sits while you are pushing it through fabric. Another style thimble that is useful for pushing needles is a flat metal piece with a dimpled surface on the end. (Note that a small uninflated balloon can produce a good grip when folded around a needle and may work better than a thimble in some cases. You can also use a piece of soft leather or rubber fingertips.)

- *Alligator clips* come in two styles, one with teeth and the other with flat blades. Found in electronic and hardware stores, these are helpful for clamping strands to keep beads from sliding off. Wrap the strand around one of the jaws before closing to keep the beads in place while stringing.

- *Therapeutic gloves* are effective for relief from hand fatigue, arthritis, carpal tunnel syndrome, and other repetitive-motion disorders. As computer users know, they provide a soothing relief by reducing hand stress and cramping. The stretch fabric supports the hand and wrist, with the fingers exposed for full dexterity and free motion. See Resources for information on where to purchase these gloves.

- A *sliding pocket gauge* is a device that is useful for measuring beads when you need to know the exact size of your beads so you can string them in graduated sizes. The gauge is also useful for verifying sizes when you want to reorder specific beads.

- A *sailmaker's palm* is worn on the hand and is used for pushing a heavy needle through leather or through thick layers of sailcloth. While the palm may not work with beading needles, it is a handy tool to use when penetrating thick layers with a glover's needle.

OTHER STRINGING SUPPLIES

Appropriate threads for beading by machine are covered in Chapter 4. Select a thread for stringing that will suit your project, its use, and its wearability. Ideally, the thread should fill the hole in each bead. Use a permanent pen to write the size of the beading thread on the spool or paper bobbin so it will be easier to select the correct size for future projects. In the beginning, for each project you do you might want to record in a notebook the size of needle, thread, and beads so you can repeat or make changes without having to second-guess your own work. Your local bead shop will be helpful with classes and can make suggestions based on their stock.

You may find other stringing materials to highlight your beadwork. Sporting goods stores carry threads for tying flies. Metallic tinsel-wrapped floss is elegant when used with handmade glass beads. Stitchery shops stock an array of other cords and novelty threads that may be just right for one of your projects. Table A.1 below suggests stringing materials and when to use them for beadwork by hand. If you like pushing the limits on creativity, this information may also be helpful as you bead by machine.

Table A.1 *Bead, Thread, and Needle Combinations*

BEADS	THREAD	HAND NEEDLE	USES
Seed beads	Nylon Nymo #0-#B	#10-#12	Jewelry, fabric
Nugget chips, Czechoslovakian glass	Nylon Nymo #D-#F	#8-#12	Heavier jewelry, eyeglass straps, short leashes
Metal beads, heavy beads	Tigertail	None needed	Necklaces, hoop earrings, leashes
Pearls, semiprecious stones	Silk thread (size coordinated with bead holes)	Self-needle or twisted wire needle	Hand-knotted necklaces
Heavy beads or components	Waxed linen, sinew, Strington, monofilament, Kevlar, tigertail, foxtail	(depends on the thread) Self-needle, twisted wire needle, or none	All threads listed resist shredding, but don't use Kevlar with rough bead holes

Here is a listing of various stringing supplies and their uses:

- *Nylon thread* is widely used for stringing and for various beadwork techniques done by hand and by machine. Sizes for nylon thread range from a fine size 000 up through 00, 0, A, B, C, D, E, and F, the heaviest. Size B is commonly used as a doubled strand with seed beads; sizes D and F are widely available and are appropriate where strength is needed. Sources are not likely to stock all the sizes. Nymo is the brand name often found in nylon. It is resistant to rotting and frays less than silk. Nylon thread is most commonly found in black, white, and a few basic colors. For a "custom" color, you can color the white thread with a permanent marker before waxing the thread with beeswax. To do this, place the flat tip of the pen on top of one end of the thread and pull the length of the thread under the marker.

- *Silk thread,* like nylon, varies in sizes and colors. It is traditionally used for tying knots between pearls and other beads because it is slick and makes even, consistent knots. Over time, it stretches less than nylon. Bead suppliers carry a twisted style made specially for stringing.

- *Wax thread* is used for stringing heavy beads and large jewelry components. Wax thread may be polyester or linen. The cord is resistant to fraying (due to the wax coating) and comes in several basic colors.

- *Conso upholstery thread* is a twisted filament that is used when Nymo D isn't heavy enough. It is available in basic colors at sewing and upholstery stores. Use with size 10/0 and 11/0 beads.

- *Monofilament* is clear and is available in many weights from several sources, including sporting goods stores. Superfine monofilament used for machine beading is found with machine embroidery supplies. Nylon fishing line is stiff enough to be beaded without using a needle. Use 6- to 40-lb-test line for stringing, matching the weight to the project and bead size. Using the right weight makes a difference since a heavy line will give the jewelry a stiff look. Finish the ends with crimp beads to prevent slippage.

- *Tigertail* is a strong, flexible steel wire that is coated with nylon to prevent fraying. Although it is not as flexible as other bead cords, it is ideal for supporting stone, metal, and large or heavy beads that may have sharp edges. The four sizes are .012" (thin, 8-lb-test), .015" (10-lb-test), .019" (15-lb-test), and heavy .026" (20-lb-test). Finish the tigertail ends with crimp beads.

- *Foxtail* is a nickel chain that has a braided finish. It comes in six sizes, ranging from a light .032" (#00) to a heavy .061" (#3). It is great for stringing metal and glass beads and stretches less than any other stringing supply. Finish the ends by soldering them to the jump rings of the clasp or by joining the ends together. Always make sure to leave a little slack so the chain can flex for movement with the beads. Some beaders prefer to finish off foxtail with crimp beads instead of solder.

- *Fine brass or copper wire* (#32 gauge) is used for beaded flowers and for stringing beads onto screened discs. These perforated shapes are used for earring and brooch pads and allow for threading lots of beads in a small area with the fine wire.

- *Memory wire or spring coil* is available in two sizes: 1⅝" diameter (for bracelets) and 3½" diameter (for necklaces). For a bracelet, string beads and end by bending a loop in the wire after the last bead or by gluing the last bead on the looped end of the wire.

- *Elastic cord* is easy to use and eliminates the use of a clasp. Stretchrite prepackages black, white, and metallic colors, available in fabric stores. Put a dot of craft glue on the ends to prevent raveling while stringing beads. Tie a bead or button with an overhand knot on one end of the strand to serve as a stop. After stringing the beads, stretch the elastic, pulling out a couple inches, and knot the ends together with a square knot. Seal the knot with glue. Rainbow Elastic Plus provides 47 colors, silver, and gold, which are used for knitting, crocheting, and sewing. This soft elastic is best for lightweight beads and may be doubled when the hole is large enough.

- *Leather thong* is a thick cord appropriate for large, heavy beads. Ceramic and stone beads look good with this decorative cord in combination with decorative knotting techniques. It is available in several colors. One drawback is that it deteriorates with age.
- *Rattail* (rayon with a cotton core) and *silk cord* (silk with a nylon core) are luxurious satinlike cords used for Chinese knotting and for stringing large, artistic beads. The two sizes (#4 and #5) are less than 1/8″ thick. The ends need to be covered with a cone or some style of bead cap. Rattail is found in fabric and bead shops.

GLUES AND CEMENTS

If you are overwhelmed at the thought of selecting the correct adhesive for a project, the following information should help you sort out the options. It explains the different properties of adhesives so you can choose the right glue, cement, or epoxy for the job. Joining similar materials requires a different type of adhesive than joining dissimilar materials requires. Name brands are mentioned because of their availability and popularity among jewelry and craft designers. *The Crafter's Guide to Glues,* written by Tammy Young, is a user-friendly technical book about using glues and fusible webs.

Most of the products listed below are available at bead shops, where you will also find the shop's own recommendations for adhesives. There are numerous brands, and each manufacturer has many different glues, formulated for every kind of project. These are the types of features you will see listed on the adhesive packages: temporary bonding, permanent bonding, joins porous/nonporous surfaces, machine-washable, dry cleanable, flexible, use with rhinestones, thick, thin, quick drying, nontoxic, dishwasher-proof. You may want to experiment with various adhesives to come up with innovative ways to use them. Designers make exciting discoveries every day that manufacturers want to hear about, and we all benefit from sharing information.

Clean surfaces are essential for achieving a good bond. Nail polish remover with an acetone base is usually effective for cleaning bead and finding surfaces as well as for removing some glues before they are dry. It can sometimes be used instead of acetone or other solvents. Refer to the glue or cement manufacturer's directions. Ruined or unusable beads can be salvaged by using a bead reamer or diamond-tipped burr to remove the glue inside the hole.

Read the labels on the adhesives carefully. They will list other uses and also applicable precautions (for example, working in a well-ventilated area). Note that some adhesives will remove the silver backing from (and thus ruin) rhinestones. For most cases, acetone or nail polish remover will remove excess glue or cement from a bead. Always use the cleanup method suggested on the label.

A piece of advice was offered to me by Linda Lindsey, who has vast experience in repairing and restringing jewelry. She suggests to string and knot the jewelry so that the quality of the work relies on the technique rather than the glue. This is especially true when beading by machine. Properly securing the stitching before and after each bead is essential.

Here are some of the most common adhesives used in beading, with some of their uses and characteristics noted:

- *Clear nail polish* is a convenient and popular choice for sealing knots.
- *Craftsman's Goop* is an all-purpose adhesive that is waterproof and is safe in the washer and the dryer. It is thinner than E-6000 and made by the same company. It works well with Friendly Plastic.
- *Jewel Glue* by Delta dries clear and is machine-washable and dry cleanable (laundered garments should be air-dried to protect the beads). It is versatile for most jewelry-making needs and is very strong. Clean up the glue with water while it is still wet.
- *E-6000 bonding adhesive* is used to attach findings in costume jewelry and is good for sealing the split in jump rings. It is perfect for attaching Friendly Plastic to findings and can be used on acrylic rhinestones if you like the crackled effect on the foil backing. E-6000 is thicker than Craftsman's Goop, which is made by the same company. It dries waterproof and flexible and can join many surfaces, including plastic, rubber, glass, and metal.
- *Epoxy* produces a strong, permanent bond for nonporous materials. It is available at hardware stores and craft stores in a container that conveniently dispenses both parts of the two-part mixture simultaneously. Only a little stirring with a palette knife (or a toothpick for small amounts) is needed. Epoxy is easy to use and makes a bond as strong as soldering. The quick-drying formula is a gel that sets in about 5 minutes, while the stronger formula sets in about 30 minutes and is waterproof.
- *Germanow-Simon (G-S) Hypo-Tube Cement* was originally formulated for cementing watch crystals and for optical uses. It is not suggested as a permanent bond for jewelry, but it is recommended by professionals for fusing knots on monofilament and Nymo since it will saturate the thread and is easy to apply with its precision pinpoint applicator. Known as "G-S" or "crystal cement," it is slower drying than some other glues and thus a knot can be repositioned before it sets. G-S cleans off with alcohol and will not bond fingers like super glues. This jeweler's cement will not make thread brittle and is less likely to bond it to the inside of the beads.
- *527 cement* is a multipurpose adhesive. Its strong bond works on all surfaces. You can glue flat rhinestones or cabochons to fabric and then heat-set them with an iron when dry so they will be machine-washable.
- *Henrietta Virchick's Gum Arabic* is used to secure the knots between pearls and semiprecious beads and also to make a fine, strong thread needle or self-needle as described in Chapter 2. The knots are then waterproofed with clear nail polish. Henrietta Virchick, author of *Pearl and Bead Stringing With Henrietta,* has come up with a gum arabic that is specifically made for use on silk thread.
- *Tacky glue* is an old crafting favorite that is readily available at sewing and craft stores. If you allow it to dry long enough, it produces a surprisingly strong bond for most crafting projects. Use water for thinning and cleanup.
- *Unique Stitch* dries flexible and has a rubberlike feel. It is found in fabric stores in tubes. This glue was among the first to be used for gluing beads on garments that were machine-washable and is still a good choice today.

RESOURCES

Please check with your local sewing machine dealer, bead store, or craft store to see if they can obtain products they don't stock. When making inquiries to the companies listed below, please include a self-addressed stamped envelope. Many of the companies listed below have mail order catalogs.

BEAD CRAFTING SUPPLIES AND JEWELRY FINDINGS

Advantage Products
P.O. Box 3837
Pagosa Springs, CO 81147
(970) 731-9769
Tip-Pens

AMACO
American Art Clay Co., Inc.
4717 W. 16th St.
Indianapolis, IN 46222
(317) 244-6871
(317) 248-9300 Fax
Rub 'N Buff, Brush 'N Leaf metallic finishes

Atelier De Paris
1543 S. Robertson Blvd.
Los Angeles, CA 90035
(310) 553-6636
(213) 939-2637 (FAX)
Pendants and pins for mounting painted or embellished fabrics

B & B Products, Inc.
18700 N. 107th Avenue, Ste. 10-11
Sun City, AZ 85373
(602) 933-2962
(602) 815-9095 (FAX)
Dip 'N Etch and Etching Creme for glass beads and other uses

The Craft Beader
P.O. Box 200
Londonderry, NH 03053
The Craft Beader tool, project books, paper bead supplies

Creative Crystal Company
P.O. Box 8
Unionville, CT 06085
(800) 578-0716
BeJeweler tool, crystals, rhinestones, and metal trims

Deborah Gayle Sales
P.O. Box 402
Rodeo, CA 94572
(800) 484-9922 #8232
(510) 245-2304 (FAX)
Sewing charms, sewing machine charm/eyeglass holders, watch face with stork scissors

FeltCrafts
254 Ventura Avenue
Palo Alto, CA 94306
(800) 450-2723
Felt making kits, books, videos

Fun Foods
2 Hudson Place
Hoboken, NJ 07030
(201) 795-9416
(201) 795-3906 (FAX)
Pasta shapes (hearts, bunnies, flags, pumpkins, Christmas trees, Hanukkah, clover)

Henrietta's Beading Supply Co., Inc.
P.O. Box 260
Matawan, NJ 07747
(908) 566-3952
Video/book on pearl and bead stringing (knotting), gum arabic, supplies

K.H. Lee Tool Supply
9078 Artesia Blvd.
Bellflower, CA 90706
(800) 435-4966
Mail-order catalog available for $3 refundable with first order of $25 or more; selection of tools for jewelry making

Lilac Enterprises, Inc.
1480 Russet Drive
Eugene, OR 97401
(800) 357-6779
(503) 334-6412
Pearl Dye for dying plastics

Polychem Corp.
20 Fifth Avenue
Cranston, RI 02910
(401) 461-0500
(401) 461-0503
Paint It Pretty pens in transparent, pearl, metallic, and opaque colors for painting metal

River Gems and Findings
6901 Washington Street, NE
Albuquerque, NM 87109
(800) 443-6766
Comprehensive source for beads, tools, findings

Salis International, Inc.
4093 North 28th Way
Hollywood, FL 33020
(305) 921-6971
(305) 921-6976 (FAX)
Dr. Ph. Martin's Radiant Concentrated Water Color

The Shepherdess
2802 Juan Street
San Diego, CA 92110
(619) 297-4110
(619) 297-9897 (FAX)
Extensive classes with nationally known artists; all beading supplies and findings; Delica bead source

Tecnocraft
616 111th Street
Arlington, TX 76011
(800) 444-9051
Hi-lo temperature mini glue sticks and guns; nonstick drip pads

Universal Synergetic, Inc.
16510 S.W. Edminston Road
Wilsonville, OR 97070-9514
(503) 625-2323
(503) 625-4329
General beading supplies and classes

Wall Lenk Corporation
P.O. Box 3349
Kinston, NC 28502
(919) 527-4186
(919) 527-4189 (FAX)
Gem Tool for hot gluing rhinestones

BEAD STORAGE SUPPLIES

Dal-Craft, Inc.
P.O. Box 61
Tucker, GA 30085
(404) 939-2894
(404) 939-2070 (FAX)
Bead Caddies, Bead-Nabber, Bead Tray with covers

Dream Works, Inc.
8711-192nd Street, SE
Snohomish, WA 98290
(206) 668-8297
(206) 668-3956 (FAX)
Bead and Bauble Wheel and individual stacking containers and lids

Just Nan
2602 East 74th Place
Tulsa, OK 74136
(918) 494-0361
Bead Hive interlocking boxes with slide-out trays

OTHER SUPPLIES

Butler Brothers Watch Repair
8813 South Santa Fe Avenue
Oklahoma City, OK 73139
(405) 631-9345
Vintage watches refurbished; quartz or original workings restored

Calico Moon Handcrafts
1575 Jefferson NE
Salem, OR 97303
(800) 678-7607
(503) 399-8513 (FAX)
Fabric-covered box kits

Althea Church
38 Hancock Street
Arlington, MA 02174
(619) 641-1454
Pin Poppet Needlecase doll patterns and others

Co-Motion Rubber Stamps, Inc.
4455 S. Park Avenue, Ste. 105
Tucson, AZ 85714-1669
(800) 225-4894
(800) 852-3709 (FAX)
Precut blank greeting cards and envelopes

ConneXXions Unlimited
P.O. Box 23863
Columbia, SC 29224
(803) 736-7494
Hand-Aids support gloves

FeltCrafts
254 Ventura Ave.
Palo Alto, CA 94306
(800) 450-2723
Felt making supplies, books

Home Arts, Inc.
496 West Plumb Lane
Reno, NV
(800) 484-9923
Chipboard box kits for covering; video

Home-Sew
P.O. Box 4099
Bethlehem, PA 18018-0099
(610) 867-3833
(610) 867-9717 (FAX)
Assorted trims, braids, doll buttons

Lacis
3163 Adeline St.
Berkeley, CA 94703
(510) 843-7178
Supplies and comprehensive book selection on beadwork, embroidery

Michiko's Creations
P.O. Box 4313
Napa, CA 94558
(707) 224-8546
(707) 224-2246 Fax
All colors of Ultrasuede and Ultraleather, Japanese Washi paper

Ghee's
2620 Centenary Blvd. #2-250
Shreveport, LA 71104
(318) 222-1701
(318) 222-1781 (FAX)
Purse frames, hardware and patterns, embellishment books including beading

Patternworks
335 New Hackensack Road
Poughkeepsie, NY 12603
(800) 438-5464
Handeze therapeutic craft gloves

Watch Us, Inc.
500B Monroe Tpke., Suite 351
Monroe, CT 06468
(203) 736-0127
(203) 735-2891 (FAX)
Large assortment of watches

The Yarn Tree
P.O. Box 724
Ames, IA 50010
(515) 232-3121
(515) 232-0789 (FAX)
Glass and acrylic paperweights, precut blank greeting cards and envelopes

The Velvet Touch
908 Cyad Drive
San Marcos, CA 92069
(800) 582-4286
(619) 744-0439 (FAX)
Press 'N Wear bonding film for fabric and crafting

Your Stencil Source
P.O. Box 220
Standard, CA 95373
(800) 290-8921
(209) 533-2061 (FAX)
(209) 533-1935 Craft Castle StenSource stencils

LIGHTS AND MAGNIFIERS

EK Success Ltd.
611 Industrial Road
Carlstadt, NJ 07072-1687
(800) 524-1349
(800) 767-2963 (FAX)
Beam & Read Plus Magnifier and stand

MFD Enterprises
222 Sidney Baker South, Ste. 204
Kerrville, TX 78028
(210) 896-6060
(210) 896-6064 (FAX)
MagEye's magnifying glasses

SeldenCRAFT
37 Saddle Ridge Road
Bloomfield, CT 06002
(203) 243-1711
(203) 242-2241 (FAX)
Enlarger-Lite with magnifying lens, gooseneck extension, Lite-Foot

SCISSORS AND CUTTING TOOLS

Clover Needlecraft, Inc.
1007 E. Dominguez St., Ste. L
Carson, CA 90746
(310) 516-7846
Scallop paper scissors, wavy paper scissors, stork scissors gold charm

Dream Works, Inc.
8711-192nd Street, SE
Snohomish, WA 98290
(206) 668-8297
(206) 668-3956 (FAX)
Lift-N-Snip scissors, Lit'l Snip scissors, Slant-N-Snip scissors, Bead and Bauble Wheel, individual stacking containers and lids

Fiskars, Inc.
7811 West Stuart Ave.
Wausau, WI 54401
(715) 848-3657
(715) 848-5528 (FAX)
Paper Edgers, assorted scissors and cutting tools

Uchida of America, Corp
1027 E. Burgrove St.
Carson, CA 90746
(800) 541-5877
(310) 632-0333 (FAX)
Assortment of small and jumbo craft punches

MACHINE ACCESSORIES AND EMBROIDERY SUPPLIES

C.J. Enterprises
302 West Willis St. #105
Prescott, AZ 86301
(520) 778-0998
(602) 778-1254 (FAX)
Creative Feet: Pearls 'N Piping, Satinedge, Sequins 'N Ribbon, Accessory Guides

Clotilde
2 Smart Way B8031
Stevens Point, WI 54481-8031
(800) 772-2891
Mail order for sewing and crafting supplies (soldering iron, Fiskars Paper Edgers, Tip-Pens)

Craftco Industries, Inc.
410 Wentworth Street North Hamilton
Ontario, Canada L8L 5W3
(800) 661-0010
(905) 572-1164 (FAX)
Blue and white pounce

The Crafty Critter
Marilyn Allen
P.O. Box 16124
Duluth, MN 55816
Supplies and patterns for beading by machine

Creative Stitches
P.O. Box 17413
Salt Lake City, UT 84117
(800) 748-5144
(801) 272-3861
Mail-order machine embroidery supplies

Kreinik Metallics
1708 Gihon Road
P.O. Box 1966
Parkersburg, WV 26102
(304) 422-8900
(304) 428-4326 (FAX)
Metallic threads, cords, and braids for hand and machine embroidery; glow-in-the-dark threads in four colors

Madeira Marketing Ltd.
600 East 9th Street
Michigan City, IN 46360
(213) 873-1000
Assorted machine embroidery threads

Nancy's Notions
P.O. Box 683
Beaver Dam, WI 53916
(800) 833-0690
Sewing supplies and cross-locked beads

Rainbow Elastic Plus
P.O. Box 852
Solana Beach, CA 92075
(619) 457-3950
(619) 481-5507 (FAX)
Elastic thread in several colors; crystals

Sew-Art International
Bountiful, UT
(800) 231- 2787
Machine embroidery supplies

Speed Stitch
P.O. Box 3472
Port Charlotte, FL 33949
(813) 629-3199
Machine arts and quilting supplies

Sulky of America, Inc.
3113-D Broadpoint Drive
Harbor Heights, FL 33983
(800) 874-4115
(941) 743-4634
Machine embroidery rayon and metallic threads, stabilizers, other supplies; also training seminars

Treadleart
25834 Narbonne Ave.
Lomita, CA 90717
(310) 534-5122
Machine embroidery and quilting supplies

Tri-Star Plastics
1934 East Alosta, Ste. B
Glendora, CA 91740
(818) 335-4461
Glass beads, colored pearl beads for machine embroidery, 430 colorfast Union rayon threads

MAGAZINES

Bead & Button
P.O. Box 1020
Norwalk, CT 06856
(800) 400-2482
Techniques, projects, artists working with beads and buttons; no ads

The Crafts Report
300 Water St.
P.O. Box 1992
Wilmington, DE 19801
(800) 777-7098
A must for craft professionals; gives marketing ideas and business management tips

The Creative Machine
P.O. Box 2634-NL
Menlo Park, CA 94026
(415) 366-4440
Published to provide a link between sewing machine companies, books, events, and those who love to sew

Jewelry Crafts
4880 Market Street
Ventura, CA 93003
(805) 644-3824
  Profiles of successful jewelry
  crafters, marketing/display tips,
  projects for kids

Lapidary Journal
Devon Office Center
60 Chestnut Avenue, Suite 201
Devon, PA 19333-1312
  Ads are from companies selling
  beads and supplies, wholesale and
  retail

Ornament Magazine
P.O. Box 2349
San Marcos, CA 92079
(800) 888-8950
(619) 599-0228
  Articles on artists, ethnic arts, and
  collectibles in the art of personal
  adornment

Rock & Gem
4880 Market Street
Ventura, CA 93003
(805) 644-3824
  Topics include lapidary projects,
  rockhound info, metalsmithing,
  prospecting, and projects using
  found gemstones

Threads Magazine
63 S. Main St.
Newtown, CT 06470
(203) 426-8171
  For people who love to sew, articles
  on couture sewing, wearable art, fit-
  ting, fine detailing, and more

ASSOCIATIONS

The Bead Museum
140 S. Montezuma Street
Prescott, AZ 86303
(602) 445-2431

**The Center for the Study of
Beadwork**
Alice Scherer
(503) 249-1848

International Fabricare Institute
12251 Tech Road
Silver Springs, MD 20904
(301) 622-1900

National Polymer Clay Guild
1350 Beverly Rd., Suite 115-345
McLean, VA 22101

Society of Glass Beadmakers
8170 La Mesa Blvd.
La Mesa, CA 91941

ANNUAL BEADING EVENTS

**EMBELLISHMENT: The International
Bead & Button Show**
7660 Woodway, Suite 550
Houston, TX 77063
(713) 781-6864 Ext. 103
(713) 781-8182 (FAX)

WHERE TO LEARN

Crystal Myths, Inc.
Lewis Wilson
P.O. Box 3243
Albuquerque, NM 87190
  Glass bead making and videos

Fiber Statements
Pat Rodgers
46 Clinton Street
Sea Cliff, NY 11579
(516) 676-3342
  No-frills video with comprehensive
  information on free-motion embroidery and beading

M.J. Meade Weinig
25 Sutton Place North
New York, NY 10022
(212) 223-0231
(212) 754-5830 (FAX)
  Textile and bead conservator

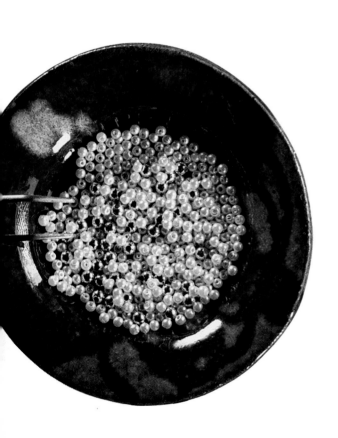

REFERENCES

BOOKS AND ARTICLES

Allen, Marilyn, *Machine Beadwork Techniques Manual,* self-published, 1994.

The Bead Museum, *The Work of Contemporary Glass Beadmakers* (color catalog of exhibits at the museum), 1993.

Benesh, Carolyn L.E., and Robert K. Liu, *The Collector's Sourcebook,* Ornament, 1995.

Benmour, Linda, *The Bead Directory,* Artstone Press, 1994.

Campbell-Harding, Valerie, and Pamela Watts, *Bead Embroidery,* Lacis, 1993.

Carter, Ginger, "Beads in American Fashion: Reflecting Our Times in Elegance," *The Flying Needle,* vol. XVII, no. 3, August 1988.

Coles, Janet, and Robert Budwig, *The Book of Beads,* Simon and Schuster, 1990.

Dodson, Jackie, *How to Make Soft Jewelry,* Chilton Book Company, 1991.

Drew-Wilkenson, Kate, with Colin Haynes, *How to Be Successful in the Bead Jewelry Business,* Nomad Press, 1993.

Francis, Peter Jr., *Beads of the World,* Schiffer Publishing, 1994.

Freed, Leba, "Beads Forever!" *The Flying Needle,* vol. XVII, no. 3, August 1988.

Hjort, Barbara, "Buttons and Beads, Bake Your Own from Polymer Clay," *Threads Magazine,* #39, Feb./March 1992.

Kohl, MaryAnn F., *Mudworks,* Bright Ring Publishing, 1989.

Liu, Robert K., *Collectible Beads: A Universal Aesthetic,* Ornament, 1995.

Moss, Kathlyn, and Alice Scherer, *The New Beadwork,* Harry N. Abrams, Inc., Publishers, 1992.

Perez-Collins, Yvonne, *Soft Gardens,* Chilton Book Company, 1994.

Roche, Nan, *The New Clay,* Flower Valley Press, 1991.

Simpson Conner, Wendy, *The Best Little Beading Book,* Interstellar Publishing Company, 1995.

Stone, Kari, "Crazy About Clay," *Jewelry Crafts,* Feb. 1994.

Thompson, Angela, *Embroidery with Beads,* Lacis, 1992.

Vickrey, Anne, *FeltCrafts,* Craft Works Publishing, 1987.

Young, Tammy, *Crafter's Guide to Glues,* Chilton Book Company, 1995.

VIDEOS

Campbell-Harding, Valerie, and Pamela Watts, *Bead Embroidery,* 1993.

Rodgers, Pat, *Free Motion Machine Embroidery and Beading By Machine,* 1993.

Virchick, Henrietta, *Pearl & Bead Stringing With Henrietta,* 1987.

Wilson, Lewis, *Glass Beadmaking* series, #1, 2, 3, 4.

INDEX